Essays on the Modern Japanese Church

MICHIGAN MONOGRAPH SERIES IN JAPANESE STUDIES
NUMBER 27

CENTER FOR JAPANESE STUDIES
THE UNIVERSITY OF MICHIGAN

Essays on the Modern Japanese Church: Christianity in Meiji Japan

Yamaji Aizan

Translated by Graham Squires, with Introductory Essays by Graham Squires and A. Hamish Ion

Ann Arbor, 1999
Center for Japanese Studies
The University of Michigan

Published by the Center for Japanese Studies, The University of Michigan
202 S Thayer St., Ann Arbor, MI 48104–1608

Library of Congress Cataloging-in-Publication Data

Yamaji, Aizan, 1865–1917
  [Gendai Nihon kyōkai shiron. English]
  Essays on the modern Japanese church : Christianity in Meiji
Japan / Yamaji Aizan ; translated by Graham Squires ; with intro-
ductory essays by Graham Squires and A. Hamish Ion.
    p. cm. — (Michigan monograph series in Japanese studies ; 27)
  Includes bibliographical references and index.
  ISBN 0-939512-93-9 (alk. paper)
    1. Japan—Church history—19th century. 2. Japan—Religion—
1868–1912. I. Squires, Graham, 1955– . II. Ion, A. Hamish.
III. Title. IV. Series.

BR1307.Y3613 1999
275.2'08—dc21   99–047907

This book was set in Caslon 540.

Jacket design by Seiko Semones

This publication meets the ANSI/NISO Standards for Permanence of Paper
for Publications and Documents in Libraries and Archives (Z39.48–1992).

Printed in the United States of America

CONTENTS

PREFACE

Yamaji Aizan's *Essays on the History of the Modern Japanese Church* was first published in 1906. It is significant for two reasons. First, Yamaji was one of the most influential historians of the mid-Meiji period, and it is one of his most important works. This is reflected in the fact that, of all his books and essays, it is the one which has been most often reprinted in Japanese. Second, it was the first history of the Protestant Church in Meiji Japan, and as such it has done much to set the tone for subsequent studies of this subject. The objective of this translation is to make this work available to a wider audience and thereby to enhance understanding of both Yamaji's life and thought and the history of Meiji Christianity.

In order to render a historical work from one language into another, it is insufficient merely to translate the text word by word, sentence by sentence, page by page. The audience for which the original text was written and the audience for which the translation is written are clearly quite different. For a historical text to have meaning for a modern audience it is necessary for that text to be located within an appropriate "context." In the case of *Essays*, it can be located within two distinct contexts—one is the life and thought of Yamaji Aizan and the other is the historiography of Meiji Christianity. The objective of the first introductory essay is to give an overview of Yamaji Aizan's life and thought and to relate this to some of the key elements in his *Essays*. In the second introductory essay, Professor A. Hamish Ion of the Royal Military College of Canada, Ontario, Canada, examines Yamaji's position within Meiji Christianity and locates *Essays* within the historiography of Meiji Protestantism.

I would like to acknowledge the assistance of Dr. Yushi Ito, Victoria University of Wellington, New Zealand, for the help he so kindly provided as supervisor during my doctoral candidacy; Professor Fred G. Notehelfer, University of California, Los Angeles, for reading and commenting on earlier drafts of the manuscript; and the staff at the Center for Japanese Studies, University of Michigan, for the effort they made in preparing the final version of this book. Finally, I would like to thank my parents, Peggy and Russell Squires, for their support and encouragement over many years.

Graham Squires
June 1999

Introductory Essays

YAMAJI AIZAN AND *ESSAYS ON THE HISTORY OF THE MODERN JAPANESE CHURCH*

Graham Squires

Yamaji Yakichi—Aizan was a pen name adopted when he was around twenty years old—was born in 1864 in the mansion of the Astronomical Institute of the Tokugawa shogunate located in Edo.[1] The Yamaji were one of the four families that held the hereditary post of official astronomers to the shogunate. Following the abolition of the institute after the Meiji Restoration, however, Yamaji moved to Shizuoka together with his grandparents in the spring of 1869. This move involved not only the Yamaji family but many other former retainers of the Tokugawa, who moved there as a part of the political settlement following the Restoration. As a young child Yamaji was educated by his grandparents, but in 1874 he began to attend a local school. By 1878, however, the family was no longer able to afford the tuition fees, so he changed from being a student to working as a teacher at the same school. In 1881 he became a clerk in the police department and in 1882

---

1. The most detailed studies of Yamaji's life and thought have been undertaken by Ōka Toshiro and Sakamoto Takao. A collection of Ōka's most important essays has recently been published under the title, Ōka Toshiro, *Yamaji Aizan, shironka to seijironka no aida* (Tokyo: Kenbun Shuppan, 1998). Sakamoto's works include "Yamaji Aizan no shisō—toku ni zenhanki no katsudo o chushin to shite," *Gakushuin Daigaku hōgakubu kenkyū nenpō* 20 (1985): 105–311; "Yamaji Aizan no seiji shisō." *Gakushuin Daigaku hōgakubu kenkyū nenpō* 21 (1986): 103–309; and *Yamaji Aizan* (Tokyo: Yoshikawa Kobunkan, 1988). In Western languages Margaret Neuss has published "On the Political Thinking of Yamaji Aizan" in *Tradition and Modern Japan*, ed. P. G. O'Neill (Kent: Paul Norbury, 1981), 93–101, and "Zur Rolle de Heldenbiographien im Geschichtsbild Miyake Setsureis und Yamaji Aizans," *Oriens Extremus* 25.1 (1978): 1–44.

started to attend a local English school part-time, where he studied the work of John Stuart Mill and Herbert Spencer. In 1884, with a group of friends, he began to study English conversation at the local Methodist Church, and in 1885 the entire group converted to Christianity. Yamaji himself was baptized in March 1886.

In February 1887, Yamaji read, and was greatly impressed by, the first edition of the *Kokumin no tomo*. As is well known, this journal was published by the Min'yūsha, a publishing company established by Tokutomi Sohō. In 1889 Yamaji moved to Tokyo to study at the school of the Methodist Church, the Tōyō Eiwa Gakkō, and while in Tokyo he had the opportunity to visit the office of the Min'yūsha and meet Tokutomi. In July 1890 Yamaji moved to Fukuroi in Shizuoka to work as an "assistant pastor." While there, at the recommendation of Tokutomi, he began to read the work of Thomas Carlyle and Ralph Waldo Emerson. It was also at this time that he began contributing articles to journals such as Iwamoto Yoshiharu's journal, *Jogaku zasshi* (Journal of Women's Study). While in Fukuroi, Yamaji's writing came to the attention of leaders of the church, and in July 1891 he returned to Tokyo to become editor of the Methodist journal *Gokyō* (Defender of the Faith).

In August 1891 Tokutomi invited Yamaji to become a writer for the Min'yūsha. This appointment established Yamaji as a writer of national significance at a time when journalism was developing as a cultural phenomenon of great importance. Following the Meiji Restoration and the introduction to Japan of printing technology using movable type, there was a boom in the publishing industry. Initially newspapers and journals tended to be of one of two types. On the one hand, there were popular newspapers that were rather salacious and that aimed at making a profit. On the other hand, there were elitist papers that focused on politics and were not so much concerned with making money. As the establishment of a constitutional system approached in the late 1880s, there appeared a new kind of publication that sought to deal with important issues but that also attempted to establish a wide circulation. The publishing activity of the Min'yūsha can be seen as being representative of this trend. The *Kokumin no tomo* was not only concerned with politics; it also sought to attract a broad readership through featuring articles on all aspects of society, culture, and literature.[2] In a political sense the *Kokumin no tomo* was one of the first so-called "independent" journals.[3] Here the word "independent" means a journal that espoused a coherent set of principles and participated in the intellectual world as an advocate of those beliefs. They differed from modern journals or newspapers in that they did not claim to be impartial or to merely represent public opinion. They self-consciously tried to lead public opinion on the basis of the principles they espoused. These principles, however, did not mean simply the private opinions of the editor. On the contrary, these journals claimed to transcend factional or sectional interests, and they based their role in the intellectual world in the idea of the people. By addressing themselves directly to the people and by justifying their existence in terms of their relationship to the people, such independent publications sought to legitimize their opposition to and criticism of the Meiji government. Moreover, at the time, the world of newspapers and magazines offered young intellectuals a new freedom and a chance for success and fame outside the restrictive social system because it had few connections with the established academic, bureaucratic, business, and military cliques. In the late 1880s and the 1890s journalists and writers formed a semi-independent community that exerted a certain type of cultural influence and came to be one of the main features of the Meiji intellectual scene.[4]

In January 1893 Yamaji published a short biography of Rai San'yō in *Kokumin no tomo* entitled "San'yō o ronzu" (On Rai San'yō). This essay sparked a debate with Kitamura Tōkoku who had just established a new literary magazine entitled *Bungakukai* (Literary World) with Shimazaki Tōson and others. The theme of this debate was encapsulated in the title of one of Kitamura's essays,

2. For a description of the *Kokumin no tomo*, see John D. Pierson, *Tokutomi Sohō 1863–1957: A Journalist for Modern Japan* (Princeton: Princeton University Press, 1980), 164–77.
3. Ariyama Teruo, *Meijiki ni okeru "Kokumin shinbun" to Tokutomi Sohō* (Tokyo: Nihon Zusho Sentaa, 1988), 3–6.
4. Irene Powell, *Writers and Society in Modern Japan* (Tokyo: Kodansha International, 1983), 8.

"Jinsei ni aiwataru to wa nan no ii zo" (What Does it Means to Benefit the World?). It is in connection with this debate that Yamaji's name is principally remembered today.

After six years, in 1897, Yamaji left the Min'yūsha, and after working for a short time in the archives of the Mori family, he joined the staff of the *Shinano mainichi shinbun* (The Shinano Daily News) based in Nagano Prefecture. While in Nagano, Yamaji continued to contribute to national journals, and the content of his writing reflects his increasing concern about social inequality within Japan and about the increasing foreign threat to Japan caused by Western imperialism. In January 1903 he began publishing his own journal, *Dokuritsu hyōron* (Independent Review). He continued to publish this journal, in one form or another, until his death in 1917. While Yamaji was publishing *Dokuritsu hyōron*, he also wrote a large number of monographs. These included works such as *Shakaishugi kanken* (A Personal View of Socialism, 1906) and *Gendai kinken shi* (The Power of Money in Modern Japanese History, 1908). An outstanding feature of Yamaji's work was the large number of biographies he produced. These included biographies of Ogyū Sorai (1893), Arai Hakuseki (1894), Takayama Hikokurō (1900), Confucius (1905), Ashikaga Takauji (1909), Minamoto Yoritomo (1909), Katayama Kiyomasa (1909), Saigō Takamori (1910), Katsu Kaishu (1911), Minamoto Tametomo (1913), Iwasaki Yatarō (1913), and Tokugawa Ieyasu (1915). In addition to writing, Yamaji also gave lectures on Japanese intellectual and social history at private colleges such as Dōshisha, Keio and Waseda. Toward the end of his life he began writing *Nihon jinmin shi* (A History of the Japanese People), which he intended to be the culmination of his life's work, but this was left unfinished at the time of his death. Yamaji died at the relatively young age of fifty-two in March 1917 of complications brought on by dysentery.

In his twenty-six-year career as a writer, Yamaji produced a huge number of books and essays on a great variety of subjects. One problem in trying to understand his thought is that he did not write a single work in which he summarized his world view. Rather his ideas are scattered in many places. Despite the diver-

sity in Yamaji's writings, however, it is possible to identify a coherent world view that influenced his approach to the individual
topics he took up. In order to understand any one of Yamaji's works,
it is necessary to locate that work within the context of his overall
oeuvre. Failure to do this will lead to a distortion or misunder-
standing of his position. Perhaps the clearest example of this is
the way Yamaji has been treated in regard to his well-known debate with Kitamura Tōkoku. This debate began in 1893 when Kitamura took exception to a statement in the opening paragraph of
Yamaji's biography of Rai San'yō in which he asserted that "writing is an enterprise." Kitamura criticized Yamaji for what he took
to be his utilitarian interpretation of the role of literature. The
debate continued for several months in the pages of a number of
different journals and inspired some of Kitamura's most important essays. As a consequence, in subsequent studies of this controversy attention has focused largely on Kitamura's perspective
since he is regarded as being one of the most important figures in
the development of literature in the Meiji period.[5] Until recently
there has been a tendency to neglect Yamaji's position and accept
Kitamura's criticism at face value. From the very beginning, however, Yamaji insisted that Kitamura had misunderstood what he
was trying to say.[6]

One of the key elements in Yamaji's thought was the clear
distinction he made between the spiritual and the material worlds.
Yamaji belonged to the so-called *bunmeishi* or "history of civilization" style of historical writing, whose best-known exponent was
Taguchi Ukichi. Yamaji greatly admired Taguchi and like him
analyzed history in terms of very broad, long-term trends focus-
ing on the material aspects of human civilization. Here, "material" means not simply economic factors but also inherited social,
intellectual, literary, and religious customs and traditions. For example, in one of Yamaji's early works entitled "Kinsei busshitsu-
teki no shinpō" (Material Progress in the Early Modern Period),
Yamaji took up two of Taguchi's themes, the role of ordinary people

5. For an English language account of this debate, see Francis Mathy, "Kitamura Tōkoku:
    Essays on the Inner Life," *Monumenta Nipponica* 19 (1964): 66–110.
6. "Meiji bungakushi," *Kokumin shinbun*, 1 March–11 June 1893.

in history and the advance in material wealth. In this work he describes the importance that contact with foreign countries had on the development of Japan. He lists forty-nine examples between 1541 and 1849 of the way in which the introduction of foreign products influenced the lives of the Japanese people. One of these examples was the introduction of cotton, about which he wrote: "If the reader can understand that the struggle between cotton and silk was more important to the Japanese people than the struggle between the two armies at Sekigahara, then he can understand the importance of foreign commerce for the ordinary people."[7]

Yamaji believed, however, that above and beyond the material aspects of human existence there was a spiritual realm. He felt that because individuals had a spiritual dimension and had free will, they had the power to change the material world and hence the power to change history. He wrote that historical facts could be arrived at in two ways: facts could be deduced from laws, and laws could be induced from facts. In the final analysis, however, both methods rest on the assumption that "all human hearts are but one." Further, "for the historian, the first principle must be that all people, in the same circumstances and with the same disposition, act in the same way." With regard to the problem of how free will could act in a world governed by fixed laws, he argued that this was something that could not be known: "This is a secret. This is mysterious. This, according to the mystics, is something hidden behind the veil." Yamaji argued that history was a science because it was concerned with cause and effect, it contained premises and conclusions, and it taught laws and principles. "History is a science," he wrote, "but it is also a religion. It teaches the secret relationship between God's will and human affairs."[8]

Yamaji brought together his ideas about the role of materialism and spiritualism in history through his concept of the individual. On the one hand, he recognized the power of the material world to control individuals. On the other hand, Yamaji also recognized the power of individuals to change the material world.

7. *Kokumin no tomo*, 23 October–13 December 1892.
8. "Shigaku-ron," *Kokumin shinbun*, 20 July 1900.

Individuals could do this because they possessed free will or "spirit," which could not ultimately be suppressed by external factors. It was through actions, such as wielding a sword or pen, that individuals could transform human spirit into a form that could change the material world. It was this belief that lay behind his assertion that "writing is an enterprise." Although this passage has often been quoted, Yamaji's real meaning has largely been overlooked. In making this assertion Yamaji was not primarily concerned with how to evaluate literature but with how to understand historical individuals. He argued that, in evaluating an individual in history, attention must be paid to the way that person influenced the world. The subject of the particular essay was Rai San'yō, a writer, and so Yamaji argued that it was necessary to evaluate the way his writing influenced the world. Yamaji wrote a great many biographies, and it was his belief in the individual's ability to fight against society and to change history that lay behind his interest in biography as an analytical tool.

Yamaji also held a cyclical view of history in which societies went through successive periods of innovation and vitality followed by periods in which they gradually stagnated and became increasingly rigid. When this process of "mummification" reached such a stage that societies were no longer able to respond to people's needs, some great individual would arise and overthrow the existing order. This great individual would rejuvenate society and establish a new way of doing things. After their death, however, society would once again begin to stagnate. In an essay on the development of human rights in Japan he wrote that "It is always the case . . . that what in the beginning is a merit at the end becomes an obstacle to the advance of civilization."[9] Yamaji argued that this cycle had repeated itself a number of times in Japanese history. The end of the Heian period was a period of stagnation, which had lead to the rise of Minamoto Yoritomo. The decline of the Muromachi bakufu had led to the rise of Oda Nobunaga, Toyotomi Hideyoshi, and finally Tokugawa Ieyasu. The decline and stagnation of the Tokugawa system had led to the

9. "Nihon no rekishi ni okeru jinken hattatsu no konseki," *Kokumin no tomo*, 9–23 January 1897.

rise of Saigō Takamori and the other figures who brought about the Meiji Restoration.[10]

With regard to contemporary society also, Yamaji was concerned about the increasing degree of social inflexibility. Yamaji himself had grown up at a time immediately following the Meiji Restoration, when society was extremely open and fluid. This was a time when gifted people could make a good position for themselves simply through their own ability. As the government put in place those institutions necessary for the functioning of a modern state, however, the opportunities for advancement became increasingly limited and more dependent on formal qualifications. In 1897 the Higher Civil Service Examination was established as the principal mode of entry into the bureaucracy. On the one hand, this system ensured that those employed by the government had the administrative ability necessary for their work. On the other hand, it meant that entry into the social elite became increasingly restricted. To pass the Higher Civil Service Examination it was necessary to have a specialist knowledge of law and administration. To acquire such knowledge it was necessary to study in the Law Faculty of Tokyo University. Yamaji argued, however, that the number of people who could enter the university and become part of the elite was obviously restricted.[11] He believed that talented people could be found at all levels of society, but the number of people who had the financial assets necessary to attain higher education was limited. Thus, some young people, even though they work in a law court, "have unfortunately never passed through the gate of the university and cannot enter the Ministry of Justice because they cannot brandish some legal treatise they have written full of secondhand knowledge and boast of their erudition" and in no time "sink into the obscurity of petty officialdom." In contrast to this, students who have graduated from the university and who are so inexperienced that "they cannot tell when a potato is boiled" are picked out quickly and given important work. This situation threw a dark shadow over the future of those young

10. "Senrei sensei no fukkatsu," *Kokumin no tomo*, 10 October 1897.
11. "Gakko hekigai no seinen," *Shinano mainichi shinbun*, 2 May 1899.

people "outside the school gate" who were trying to make their way in the world through their own efforts. If a gap developed in the quality of life between those who had the family resources to procure higher education and those who did not, it would mean that society had once again become elitist. Such elitism stood in direct opposition to the kind of egalitarian society Yamaji took to be the ideal.

For Yamaji this problem went beyond the personal unhappiness of those young people who were denied access to higher education, for he was also concerned with the intellectual quality of the administrative elite. He felt that the kind of study carried out at the university simply encouraged the memorization of examination answers for the sake of graduation. In other words, what was instilled in the students was mechanical learning, and, as a result, knowledge acquired in such a way was regarded as a kind of all-embracing principle. This in turn led to a narrow outlook on life and a lack of flexibility. Put another way, the kind of education acquired at the university stunted the intellectual development of those who were to become the administrative elite.

What was true of education was also true of other aspects of society. Increased social inequality especially had been brought about by the process of industrialization that Japan had recently undergone. Yamaji believed that it was necessary for the state to intervene to counter this trend. For this reason he came to believe in what he termed *kokka shakaishugi* or "state socialism." In works such as *Shakaishugi no kanken* (A Personal View of Socialism) published in 1906, he argued that many people were frightened of the word "socialism" and thought it something new and dangerous. According to Yamaji, however, a form of socialism had existed in ancient Japan. "The state was not simply a tool that one class used to oppress another," he wrote of that time, because the "fundamental belief of this age was that the state was like a large family." Members of the imperial family were like the parents in this family, and the people were like the children. Members of the family shared a "communal life." As a result of this familial relationship, human relations within the state were not based simply on law or expediency but also had an emotional and moral aspect. Members of the family were not free simply to exploit each other but had a moral responsibility to care for one another. In practical terms, the socialist nature of these beliefs had led to policies such as the freeing of the people, the communal ownership of land and wealth, and even the implementation of some social welfare policies.

As far as contemporary society was concerned, Yamaji did not see a contradiction between the active role of the state and his emphasis on the freedom of the individual.[12] On the one hand "the state exists for the individual and on the other hand the individual exists for the state." Speaking from the perspective of the state, Yamaji wrote, it "came into existence for the people." The power of the state should be used to preserve public peace and advance the happiness of the people. The state, which is "the mother and father of the people," cannot take "the life of even one person lightly and throw it away." Speaking from the point of view of the people, however, "They were born to support the prosperity of the state and strengthen the state for eternity." For this reason, "when it reaches the point where the existence of the state is in danger, it is natural to fight and even die for the state without hesitation."[13]

It was as a result of such beliefs that Yamaji gradually became a believer in "imperialism." As is well known, as early as 1894 Tokutomi Soho had come to support an aggressive foreign policy and the adoption of policies necessary to make Japan a strong military power. Although Yamaji supported the government's policy at the time of the Sino-Japanese War, he had reservations about territorial expansion and Japan becoming a world power. He regarded these policies as those of the despotic Satsuma-Choshu clique, which dominated the government. As the 1890s progressed, however, he began to feel that Japan's position was being threatened by the encroachment of Western nations. As a consequence, in the early editions of *Dokuritsu hyoron* Yamaji argued that "people have the right to exist" and that imperialism was nothing more than the form of social organization best suited

12. "Kokkashugi to kojinshugi," *Shinano mainichi shinbun*, 4–6 July 1900.
13. Ibid.

to ensure the survival of the individual.[14] Yamaji wrote that he still believed in the freedom of the individual but that in order to maintain that freedom it was necessary to have a strong state because "there is only one institution that can defend the freedom of the individual, and that is the state." For the state to continue to exist, it was necessary for it to have the structure and resources necessary to be able to compete with the other powers. Internally, this meant putting in place the institutional framework that would allow the state to efficiently exploit Japan's resources, and, externally, it meant the acquisition of more resources through territorial expansion. For Yamaji the only way to protect the freedom of the individual was through the maintenance of a strong state, and for this reason individuals must be prepared to sacrifice themselves to protect the state. Yamaji thus strongly supported an aggressive policy toward Russia at the time of the Russo-Japanese War.

It was about the time of the Russo-Japanese War that Yamaji wrote *Essays on the History of the Modern Japanese Church*. In terms of research on the life and thought of Yamaji Aizan, this work is very significant because it provides valuable information on the way Yamaji perceived the social and intellectual world in which he lived. Although it cannot be described as an autobiographical work, it is an account of an intellectual movement in which Yamaji himself was involved, and for this reason it is very personal. Although *Essays* was first published as a book in 1906, the first half had previously appeared in serial form in *Dokuritsu hyōron* in 1904.[15] This early version was published under the title "Gendai shisoshi ni okeru Kirisutokyō no ichi" (The Place of Christianity in Modern Intellectual History) or "Nihon shisoshi ni okeru Kirisutokyō no ichi" (The Place of Christianity in the Japanese Intellectual World). As the title suggests, *Essays* is a history of the Protestant Church in Meiji Japan, but, as the alternative title also indicates, it is also an intellectual history of the Meiji period written from

---

14. "Yo wa naze ni teikokushugi no shinja taru ya," *Dokuritsu hyōron*, 1 January 1903 and "Yo ga iwayuru teikokushugi," *Dokuritsu hyōron*, 1 February and 3 March 1903.
15. This translation is based on the version contained in *Tokutomi Sohō, Yamaji Aizan, Nihon no meicho* 40, ed. Sumiya Mikio (Tokyo: Chūō Kōronsha, 1971).

the perspective of Christianity.[16] The first half, from the introduction to chapter twenty-six, covers the period from just before
the Meiji Restoration up until the late 1880s, when the journals
Kokumin no tomo and *Jogaku zasshi* were first published. In other
words, the first half of the book covers the period from around the
time Yamaji was born until about the time when he first went to
Tokyo in 1889. This was the formative period in Yamaji's intellectual development. The second half of the work was added when
Essays appeared in book form some two years later. This latter
half deals with the period from around 1890 until around 1905,
when Yamaji was active as a writer and participant in the events
he describes. In many ways, the first half of *Essays* can be seen as
an account of the intellectual forces that shaped Yamaji's development as a thinker, while the second half is a description of the
social and intellectual world in which Yamaji functioned as an adult.

Kenneth Pyle has argued that young intellectuals of the
mid-Meiji period experienced an identity crisis. They wanted to
accept the new culture of the West, but such acceptance seemed
to require them to abandon their own Japanese culture.[17] Reading
through the early part of *Essays*, however, we can see that Yamaji's
principal concern was not with polarities between Japan and the
West but with conflicting spiritual and material values. This conflict took three distinct forms. Within the Sino-Japanese intellectual tradition there was the spiritualism of the Wang Yang-ming
school and the materialist strand of thought represented by Yasui
Sokken. Within the newly introduced forms of Western thought
there was the spiritualism of Christianity and the materialism of
Spencer and Darwin as interpreted by Katō Hiroyuki, Toyama
Masakazu, and Edward Morse at Tokyo University. Finally, there
was Yamaji's interpretation of the social consequences of the Meiji
Restoration. It is this aspect of *Essays* that is of most interest because it most clearly reflects Yamaji's own personal experience.

In *Essays* Yamaji described the Meiji Restoration as a "general revolution" and as "a fundamental revolution that passed

16. Imanaka Kanshi, "Yamaji Aizan no shisō to Kirisutokyō: Nihon shisō ue ni okeru
    Kirisutokyō no ichi," *Kirisutokyō shakai mondai kenkyū* 11 (1967): 169–96.
17. *The New Generation in Meiji Japan: Problems of Cultural Identity 1885–95* (Stanford:
    Stanford University Press, 1969), 4.

through both the spiritual and material aspects of society." He believed that the Meiji Restoration occurred because Tokugawa society had become moribund, and in this regard, the leaders of the Restoration had achieved a great task. He wrote that "the men of Satsuma and Choshu had a great mission in Japanese history. Now they have accomplished that mission." Although the leaders of the Restoration had provided a great service in bringing about the end of the shogunate, their role in post-Restoration society was not so positive.

In a political sense Yamaji was a fundamental opponent of the Meiji oligarchs, and this was linked to his own personal background. As noted earlier, Yamaji was born just four years before the Restoration into an elite family in the service of the shogunate. Following the Restoration, however, Yamaji's family moved to Shizuoka along with many other retainers of the Tokugawa. Those who moved to Shizuoka experienced considerable hardship, however, for the government had cut off traditional forms of payment and the retainers were obliged to move there without any financial assistance. After arriving in Shizuoka they became known as *o-tomari-san* or "lodgers" because, lacking any place to stay, they were obliged to lodge in temples, private houses, and other temporary accommodations. In material terms the former Tokugawa retainers may not have been very well off, but culturally they were the elite of Edo society. Although Shizuoka was a provincial center, it was suddenly filled with refugees from the capital, and this had a profound impact on the area after the Restoration. It was in these circumstances that the Yamaji family moved there. The move naturally changed Yamaji's life although he later wrote that he could not remember much of the actual trip: "I cannot help but think of Shizuoka as my hometown. I was not born in Shizuoka but for twenty years I grew up there."[18]

In the early 1890s Yamaji wrote two autobiographical novels describing his life in Shizuoka.[19] The first largely deals with relations within his own family; the second deals extensively with

18. Quoted in Ōka, "Shizuoka jiken to Yamaji Aizan," *Shizuoka ken kindaishi kenkyūkai kaihō* 12 (1983): 1.
19. Yamaji Aizan, *Jinsei, mei ka tsumi ka,* ed. Ishigami Ryōhei and Ishigami Hiroko (Tokyo: Eishobo, 1985).

the social experience of the former shogunate retainers in Shizuoka. In this second novel, Yamaji emphasizes the differing fates of the "victors" and the "vanquished" in the Meiji Restoration. In fact, reading through this work, one cannot help but be struck by the degree of bitterness Yamaji felt toward Satsuma and Choshu. He complained that the children of the victors in the Restoration had every advantage that money could buy and that those who were on the losing side had nothing. This, he complained, had nothing to do with their respective merit. "I was thrown into the world of the despised Shizuoka samurai," he wrote, "so I can easily understand the fate of the vanquished. . . . I have experienced a taste that the victors have not experienced. Not just me but all those despised as the 'stupid retainers of the Tokugawa' have experienced this taste. The taste of bile is bitter."[20] Although the precise degree of hardship experienced by the Yamaji family is open to question, we cannot doubt that in comparison with their former wealth and status, the family experienced hardship and that Yamaji was acutely sensitive to this.

As Conrad Totman has pointed out, after the Restoration, there developed a strong "Meiji bias" in the way the events of the 1860s were interpreted by both former participants and by other writers.[21] In the memoirs of many participants, Totman writes, there are many scornful references to "the fudai daimyo," "bakufu officials," and "liege vassals." The supporters of the bakufu were portrayed as unimaginative, selfish, and unworthy, who through their ineptness rather than their dangerous ability damaged the imperial house and wrecked the unity of the court, bakufu, and lords. Moreover, the ideological position the leaders of the Restoration took in the 1860s, and the political strategies they employed after the Restoration, discouraged the creation of a literature in which they glorified themselves by lionizing those whom they had defeated. Many of those that came to support the imperial side in the final stages of the Restoration had long associations with one or another part of the vanquished side. To avoid

20. Ibid., 201.
21. Ōka, "Kaisetsu," in *Yamaji Aizan-shū II*, ed. Oka Toshiro (Tokyo: Sanichi Shobō, 1985), 344.

alienating these supporters the victors avoided glorifying themselves and instead tried to heal the wounds by reducing the visibility of the whole event and treating the Restoration as a national triumph of imperial virtue over decadence and petty vice. One consequence of this strategy was to encourage later generations of historians to minimize the violence and war involved in the Restoration and to stress instead the relative absence of upheaval and conflict. The desire of some former Tokugawa supporters to rehabilitate their own careers also led them to try and distance themselves from the bakufu and to emphasize the purity of their intentions.[22] *Essays* is of interest because it is quite clearly written from the perspective of one of those who felt he was on the losing side in the Restoration.

Yamaji approvingly quotes Fukuzawa Yukichi's assertion that Christianity gained support principally among the children of those groups who had lost out in the Restoration. These people, he argued, had little chance of success in the material world and so sought alternative values in the spiritual world. Yamaji compares and contrasts the materialism of Itō Hirobumi flirting with a shop assistant in Paris with the spiritualism of Niijima Jō praying silently in a secret room. Although Yamaji gives members of both the Yokohama Band and the Kumamoto Band as examples of those who turned to Christianity because they could not share in the material success of the new era, there can be little doubt that this assertion was based on his own experience and feelings.

In *Essays* Yamaji writes that human beings need to have their spiritual needs met in the same way as their physical needs. In the early Meiji period, he argues, there was a crisis because these needs were not being met. He analyzes the conservative reaction against the Westernization of society in the 1880s primarily in spiritual terms. Although people had grown tired of the pantheism of neo-Confucianism, they were not satisfied with the new learning of the West. Yamaji gives numerous examples of the lax behavior of people in the early Meiji period and attributes

22. Conrad Totman, *The Collapse of the Tokugawa Bakufu, 1862–1868* (Honolulu: University of Hawaii Press, 1980), 358–64.

this to the fact that they were "sceptical, materialist, and lacking in belief." The newly introduced Western forms of thought taught political rights, empiricism, and science, but unlike Confucianism and Buddhism "it did not teach life; it did not teach the way of heaven." As a result of this, Yamaji argued, it was "not to be regretted that at this time, in a part of society, there was a revival of Buddhism and Confucianism that taught human behavior, life, and moral authority." Yamaji also analyzes this phenomenon in generational terms. The generation to which Fukuzawa Yukichi belonged were like people who had just moved into a new house. They were concerned with material issues and did not have time to sit down and consider metaphysical problems.

In the late 1880s Yamaji felt that Christianity could provide a new set of values that could meet the needs not only of the individual but also of society in general. In an essay published in 1890, he stressed the need to supplement the material development that had taken place since the Restoration with corresponding spiritual development. He begins by recognizing the tremendous change that Japan had experienced since the arrival of Perry. The Diet, "unprecedented among the yellow races," had met; railways had been constructed; and laws had been established to protect rights and property. "In past or present, East or West, where is there a country like ours that has advanced so quickly and boldly?" He notes that there had been opposition to these developments. There was a time when Katō Hiroyuki had argued that it was too early to establish a parliamentary form of government. There had also been a period when the Ministry of Education had ordered schools throughout the country to revive the Confucian classics. Yamaji compared Japanese civilization to a boat in a fast-flowing river. Its fate was half in the hands of the people on board and half in the vicissitudes of the current. All Japanese were in the same position, however, so Buddhists and Christians, young and old, should work together. He next went on to warn against what he regarded as the superficial nature of Japan's progress. Although there had been great advances since the Restoration, it was merely material progress: smoking cigarettes, playing the piano, wearing frock coats, and so on. There was the danger, however, that the price for this material progress would be the loss of the dignity of the people and the destruction of the country. Having railways, a parliament, and a constitution were of no use if the way of thinking of the people who used these things was the same as the people in the feudal age. Merely having the forms of material culture was of no use if there were not the spiritual values to go with them: "The machines we already have are sufficient and the resources are also prepared. Japan now lacks the people who can use these things." Yamaji felt that the most important job for Japan was to create a spiritual civilization that could match its material civilization. In this regard, it was necessary to train people to use the material civilization. If there were not wise parliamentarians, independent businessmen, and spirited religious leaders, the nation would not be successful.[23]

In the second half of *Essays*, Yamaji deals with two major impediments to the development of Christianty—the introduction of the "new theology" and the attack on the church by those who advocated a state-oriented education system. With regard to the first of these issues, in *Essays* Yamaji argues that the "new theology" did not pose a threat to Christianity because it was based on scientific and historical research. In Yamaji's view, however, science and religion were fundamentally different things. "Religion is like poetry," he writes, "it is not something that can be arrived at through logical analysis. . . . Religion is the experience of the human heart. It is a mystical interpretation." He believed that the controversy damaged the church because church leaders would not deal with the problem directly. In Yamaji's view the reason church leaders would not speak out was that the Japanese church depended on the foreign missionaries, and the foreign missionaries were traditionalist in their approach to theological matters. If Japanese Christians took up a position the foreign missionaries did not approve of, their source of funding would dry up.

One of the major themes in Yamaji's thinking was the emphasis he placed on intellectual "independence." In a historical sense, for example, he respected people such as Rai San'yō and

23. "Eiyu-ron," *Jogaku zasshi*, 10 January 1891.

Ogyū Sorai. In the Meiji period Rai San'yō's most famous work, *Nihon gaishi* (Unofficial History of Japan) had received harsh criticism because it contained a large number of factual errors. Yamaji defended his work, however, arguing that in the Edo period there had been two distinct styles of historical writing. The so-called "Yamanote scholars" received the patronage of the aristocracy and tended to concentrate on textual criticism. Those who did not receive aristocratic patronage and who "sold scholarship to live" wrote interesting books with appeal to laymen. Although Rai San'yō "did not write the *Unofficial History of Japan* in order to sell it," he did not receive aristocratic patronage and lived independently. From the point of view of specialists, Rai San'yō's books were crude and full of mistakes, but he was able to move people emotionally just through his literary style: "I have heard that the resolve to bring about an imperial restoration among the leaders of the Meiji Restoration was not a little aroused by San'yō's books."[24] In a similar vein, Yamaji admired Ogyū Sorai for his intellectual independence. He wrote that, just as Tokugawa Japan was divided politically into domains, so it was divided intellectually. Scholars were associated with particular domains, and students who entered a particular school tended to become disciples of that school exclusively. Sorai was opposed to this: "He recommended that scholars communicate with other schools; that they read the works of other factions and not think of it as a crime; that they tear down school walls, destroy dogmas, and communicate with anybody and read any book."[25] In this way, Yamaji greatly admired people who he believed had lived independent lives and who had fought to change society. Yamaji himself also tried to lead an independent life as an intellectual, first with the Min'yūsha, and later by establishing his own journal. In the opening editorial of *Dokuritsu hyōron* he wrote: "This is something established by my own meager efforts. I wish to discuss Prince Itō and Count Ōkuma with the same attitude I discuss Yoritomo and Ieyasu. I wish to discuss the philosophers of the Imperial University with

24. "Nihon gendai no shigaku oyobi shika," *Taiyō*, 1 September 1909.
25. Yamaji's biography of Sorai is included in *Kitamura Tōkoku, Yamaji Aizan shū, Gendai Nihon bungaku taikei* 6 (Tokyo: Chikuma Shobō, 1969), 299–333.

the same fairness as I discuss the Sophists. . . . I did not establish this magazine to help a particular political, academic, or religious faction."[26]

Perhaps the clearest expression of Yamaji's belief in independent scholarship is the contrasting attitudes he took toward Yasui Sokken and Inoue Tetsujirō in *Essays*. Although Yamaji did not agree with Yasui's attack on Christianity, he praised Yasui as a scholar who studied the Bible, who learned what he could about Christianity, and who on that basis made his criticism. In contrast, Yamaji sharply attacked Inoue for his unfairness, lack of impartiality, and poor scholarship. In studying Yamaji's life and thought, Inoue Tetsujirō is a person to whom particular attention must be paid. Yamaji regarded him as his principal opponent and repeatedly attacked his ideas over many years. Although Inoue was born a little earlier than Yamaji, he belonged to the same generation, and they shared similar interests. Like Yamaji, he rejected the materialism of people such as Katō Hiroyuki and believed that it was necessary to establish a set of spiritual values that could serve as the basis of the nation. In contrast to Yamaji, however, Inoue had a relatively orthodox academic career, studying at Tokyo University and later becoming the first professor of Japanese literature there. After his appointment he was requested by the Ministry of Education to write a commentary on the Imperial Rescript on Education. This was the first of a very large number of works Inoue wrote on the theme of *kokumin dōtoku* or "national morality."[27]

Yamaji's criticism focused on two major aspects of Inoue's thought: first, his ideas about nationality, and, second, his ideas about education. Yamaji attacked Inoue's belief in the uniqueness of the Japanese race, arguing that, because human nature was the same in all places and in all times, there was nothing special about Japanese people or their culture. Inoue argued that concepts such as Bushido were uniquely Japanese, but Yamaji coun-

---

26. "Hakkan no shui," *Dokuritsu hyōron*, 1 January 1903.
27. On Inoue's life and work, see Yamazaki Masakazu and Miyakawa Toru, "Inoue Tetsujirō: The Man and his Works," in *Philosophical Studies of Japan* (Tokyo: Japan National Commission for UNESCO, 1966) 7: 111–25; and Winston Davis, "The Civil Theology of Inoue Tetsujirō," *Japanese Journal of Religious Studies* 3 (March 1976): 5–40.

tered that the idea of loyalty contained in Bushido was simply a product of the Tokugawa period. Inoue argued that obedience to the state was also a national characteristic of the Japanese, but Yamaji denied this, writing that in the past human rights had developed in Japan just as they had in Western countries. Inoue believed that Japan's *kokutai* rested on the idea of loyalty to the throne, but Yamaji insisted that Japan possessed a spirit of freedom and tolerance that had allowed it to absorb diverse foreign influences. This spirit of tolerance and freedom, he argued, "is our *kokutai*, our imperialism, our ancestors' principle, and the anthem of our country."[28]

The second aspect of Inoue's thought that Yamaji criticized concerned education. At around the time of the Russo-Japanese War, the subject of *hanmon seinen* (anguished youth) and *tandeki seinen* (decadent youth) became a major topic of conversation among Japanese intellectuals. One of the events that first called the problem of "anguished youth" to public attention was the suicide of Fujimura Misao, an eighteen-year-old student at the First Higher School in Tokyo. In May 1903, Fujimura committed suicide by throwing himself over the Kegon Falls in Nikko, leaving behind a poem carved into a tree at the top of the falls. The poem reflected his feeling of anguish and despair. Quickly, the incident generated poetry, songs, and a novel and, most importantly, became a model for other young people. In the years between 1903 and 1908, forty successful and sixty-seven unsuccessful attempts at suicide were made at Kegon Falls alone.[29]

In *Essays*, Yamaji argues that the anguish of youth was caused by the bankruptcy of statist education. He writes that a

28. "Dai Nihon sokoku no uta," *Shinano mainichi shinbun*, 29 April 1899. For a more detailed discussion of Yamaji and Inoue's contrasting attitudes toward the issue of nationality, see Ito Yushi and Graham Squires, "Approaches to Japanese History in the Late Meiji Period: Yamaji Aizan and Inoue Tetsujirō," *New Zealand Journal of East Asian Studies* 1.1 (1993): 111–29, and idem., "A Reconsideration of the Myth of Japanese Uniqueness: Rewriting Nihonjinron," in *Japanese Society Today*, ed. Kotaku Ishido and David Myers (Rockhampton: Central Queensland University Press, 1995), 147–60.

29. On the background to this incident, see Earl H. Kinmonth, *The Self-Made Man in Meiji Japanese Thought: From Samurai to Salaryman* (Berkeley: University of California Press, 1981), 206–41; and Donald Roden, *School Days in Imperial Japan: A Case Study in the Culture of a Student Elite* (Berkeley: University of California Press, 1980).

spiritual foundation is necessary for human life, and that a statist education did not provide such a foundation. Basing education on service to the state left individuals with a spiritual vacuum that led to despair. In 1908, Yamaji published an essay in which he outlined his own view of the role of education.[30] On the one hand, there was the approach of Inoue Tetsujirō, in which the state established a fixed doctrine as the basis for national education. On the other hand, there was what he regarded as the English, laissez-faire approach to education, in which the government took no part. Yamaji wrote that, of the two approaches, he inclined toward that of Inoue Tetsujirō. He argued that it was necessary to have a state that could work to minimize internal inequality and that could maintain Japan's rights internationally. In order to achieve this, it was necessary to have an education system that would facilitate the maintenance of the state. Yamaji wrote that he agreed with Inoue on the need to have an education system that would produce good citizens. He argued, however, that education was a "technique" and not a doctrine. Also, there was a great difference between a doctrine and its implementation. While Yamaji agreed that it was necessary to have an education system that would make people loyal and supportive of the state, he thought the techniques employed by the Ministry of Education were futile.

Yamaji wrote that it was natural for young people of fourteen or fifteen to experience anguish concerning the meaning of life, as in the case of Fujiwara Misao. Until recently, however, the Ministry of Education had excluded religion from schools and taught the virtues of filial piety and statism based on the Imperial Rescript on Education. Yamaji recognized the value of the Imperial Rescript but argued that young people always experience spiritual anguish and that belief comes from within and not from external pressure. It was necessary for educationalists to pay attention to and have sympathy for this anguish. Rather than preaching nationalism and loyalty it would be better for them to prepare some techniques for dealing with the anguish of young people. In a similar vein, Yamaji argued that it was useless for teachers sim-

---

30. "Kyōiku ron jō," *Dokurtsu hyōron*, 3 July 1906, 8-29.

ply to tell students to follow the rules and not to be concerned about politics. Education was inevitably closely linked to human life, and politics was a part of human life. The reason that some students now pursued an extreme form of socialism was that for a long time they had been denied the opportunity to think about politics. It was just "the result of a failed policy that had contempt for human instinct." The reason students spent time on fantasies, fell into needless anxiety, welcomed political debate, and praised extreme forms of socialism was that educators "ignored human instinct" and employed "artificial and shabby methods." Their crime was that they did not understand the psychological disposition of the people. "They do not understand that education is a technique, not a law." Yamaji wrote that the main task of those responsible for education was to harmonize the instincts of the individual with the overall goals of society. The education of the individual could not be divorced from society because individuals were inevitably a part of it. In order to ensure their own existence and progress, state and society had to cultivate the individual instinct. The beauty of education lay in its ability to harmonize individual instincts with societal needs.

Despite problems, in the concluding sections of *Essays* Yamaji was optimistic about the future of the church in Japan. Just as he argued that material conditions had encouraged the development of Christianity in the early mid-Meiji period, so he believed that inadequacies within the statist education system, disillusionment with economic success, and Japan's increasing role in world affairs would once again create conditions suitable for the development of Christianity. If the Japanese could create their own independent church, he felt, there was no reason why Christianity could not develop. In fact, however, Yamaji's prediction was quite incorrect, for Christianity never regained the influence it had in the early Meiji period.

ESSAYS AND MEIJI
PROTESTANT CHRISTIAN HISTORY

A. Hamish Ion

During his relatively short life, Yamaji Aizan proved himself to be man of many talents: biographer, historian, journalist, and teacher. *Essays on the History of the Modern Japanese Church* presents Yamaji's view of the history of Meiji intellectual thought.[1] It shows that Japanese Protestantism was related to other forces—political, economic, and intellectual—for change during the first twenty-odd years of that era.[2] Indeed, as Cyril Powles has pointed out, most historians of modern Japan today accept Yamaji's view that the young Protestant movement was "an important factor—in its character as social critic in the transition from traditional to industrial society."[3] For anyone interested in the history of Protestant Chris-

---

1. Imanaka Kanshi, "Yamaji Aizan no shisō to Kirisutokyō: Nihon no shisō ue ni okeru Kirisutokyō no ichi," *Kirisutokyō shakai mondai kenkyū* (hereafter cited as *KSMK*) 11 (1967.3): 196.
2. Aasulv Lande, *Meiji Protestantism in History and Historiography: A Comparative Study of Japanese and Western Interpretation of Early Protestantism in Japan* (Frankfurt am Main: Verlag Peter Lang, 1989), 92. See also Imanaka, "Yamaji Aizan no shisō to Kirisutokyō," 170.
3. Cyril H. Powles, "Foreign Missionaries and Japanese Culture in the Late Nineteenth Century: Four Patterns of Approach," *North East Asia Journal of Theology* (1969): 14. To substantiate his opinion, Professor Powles cites Sumiya Mikio, *Kindai Nihon no keisei to Kirisutokyō* (Tokyo: Shinkyō Shuppansha, 1962), 137, and Maruyama Masao, *Thought and Behaviour in Modern Japanese Politics* (London: Oxford University Press, 1963), 5–6. Numerous other examples can be cited, for instance, Igarashi Akio, "Kyūbakushin no Meiji Ishin," in *Iwanami Kōza Nihon Tsūshi dai 16 kan kindai 1*, ed. Iwanami Nihon Tsūshi Henshū Iinkai (Tokyo: Iwanami Shoten, 1994), 316.

tianity in Japan,[4] *Essays* is essential reading. It was the first major Japanese-language history of Protestant Christianity in Japan and has continued to have an impact on subsequent interpretations of Meiji Christianity. As will be shown in this paper, however, recent research, especially that undertaken into Meiji Christianity at the local level, has modified and amplified some aspects of Yamaji's view of Meiji Christianity. Given the fact that *Essays* was published over ninety years ago, this might be expected.

It remains true, nevertheless, that *Essays* did much to set the tone and approach that historians, who have followed Yamaji, took in analyzing the history of Meiji Protestantism and its impact upon Japanese society. Yamaji selected a limited number of Christian groups (in particular, the Yokohama and Kumamoto Christian Bands) to come to his conclusions about Protestantism as a whole; subsequent scholars tended to followed suit. The re-

---

4. There are many general histories of Christianity in Japan. One of the most useful is still that by Ebisawa Arimichi and Ōuchi Saburō, *Nihon Kirisutokyō shi* (Tokyo: Nihon Kirisutokyōdan Shuppan Kyoku, 1971). Of great value also are Dohi Akio, *Nihon Purotesutanto Kirisutokyō shi* (Tokyo: Shinkyō Shuppansha, 1982), and Dohi Akio, *Nihon Purotesutanto Kirisutokyō shiron* (Tokyo: Kyōbunkan, 1987). A more recent study that is particularly strong in dealing with the Roman Catholic experience in Japan during the 16th and 17th centuries, as well as with issues of the 19th and 20th centuries, is Gonoi Takashi, *Nihon Kirisutokyō shi* (Tokyo: Yoshikawa Kōbunkan, 1990). An invaluable source of information about Japanese Christianity is Nihon Kirisutokyō Rekishi Dai Jiten Henshū Iinkai, ed., *Nihon Kirisutokyō rekishi dai jiten* (Tokyo: Kyōbunkan, 1988). Of standard histories in English, one of the most interesting still remains Otis Cary, *A History of Christianity in Japan: Roman Catholic, Greek Orthodox, and Protestant Missions*, 2 vols. (New York: Fleming H. Revell, 1909). Fifty years later, Otis Cary's son also produced his own less detailed history: Frank Cary, *History of Christianity in Japan* (Tokyo: Kyo Bun Kwan, 1959). The centennial year of Protestant endeavor in Japan saw the publication of a number of histories including Charles Iglehart, *A Century of Protestant Christianity in Japan* (Rutland, VT & Tokyo: Charles E. Tuttle, 1959), which set the tone for postwar writings on Protestant history, and also Winburn T. Thomas, *Protestant Beginnings in Japan: The First Three Decades 1859–1889* (Rutland, VT & Tokyo: Charles E. Tuttle, 1959). In the mid-1960s, there appeared Ernest E. Best, *Christian Faith and Cultural Crisis: The Japanese Case* (Leiden: E. J. Brill, 1966), a work that was much influenced by the ideas of Sumiya Mikio, one of the leading postwar Japanese authorities on Japanese Protestantism. Five years later came Richard H. Drummond, *A History of Christianity in Japan* (Grand Rapids, MI: William B. Eerdmans Publishing Company, 1971), a study in which the writings of Hiyane Antei, a prewar historian of Japanese Protestantism, seemed to have been the decisive influence on Drummond's view of Protestant development in Japan. The difference between Best and Drummond, and those missionary authors like the two Carys, Iglehart, and Thomas before them, was their use of Japanese materials and the influence of Japanese specialists of Christian history on their ideas.

cent broadening of research into the nature of Meiji Protestantism has itself contributed to an increased interest in Yamaji and
his Christian background.[5] Clearly, Yamaji's early Christian experiences help in understanding why certain facets of Meiji Protestantism are emphasized in *Essays* and, equally significantly, why
some seemingly important elements fail to receive due attention.
As well as briefly outlining Yamaji's Christian connections, this
paper will look at certain issues raised in *Essays* in the context of
some of the more important writings and changing interpretations
concerning Protestantism in Meiji Japan.

    Essays owes a great deal to the personal experience of
Yamaji Aizan. Yamaji was a member of the second Shizuoka Christian Band, which developed from the Young People's Group (*sei-
nenkai*) at the Japan Methodist Church in Shizuoka in 1886.[6] It
had been established in September 1874 by Davidson McDonald

---

5. See, for instance, Kawasaki Tsukasa, "Tōhoku, Aizan, Meiseki, Kandō: Oitachi to Shuk-
    kai," in *Nihon Purotesutanto shi no shosō*, ed. Takahashi Masao (Saitama Prefecture,
    Ageo City: Sei Gakuin Daigaku Shuppankai, 1995), 142–74. See also Shiori Takashi,
    "Nagano jidai no Yamaji Aizan: Purudamu jiken o chushin ni shite," in Takahashi,
    Nihon Purotesutanto shi no shosō, 175–94
6. The name Japan Methodist Church was the local name given at the insistence of
    Nakamura Masanao and Hiraiwa Yoshiyasu to the Japan District of the Methodist
    Church of Canada at its formation in September 1876. See Hiraiwa Yoshiyasu, "The
    Relation of Rev. George Cochran D. D. to the Ushigome Church," typescript, H13F4
    [52], in Victoria University-United Church of Canada archives, Toronto, Ontario,
    Canada, n.d. In addition to the Canadian Methodists, there were two American
    Methodist Episcopal missions in Meiji Japan, but they remained largely separate
    until the United Japan Methodist Church was formed in 1907. In the context of this
    essay, the Japan Methodist Church always refers to that church supported by the
    Japan Mission of the Methodist Church of Canada. For the history of the Shizuoka
    Methodist Church during this period, see Nippon Mesojisutō Shizuoka Kyōkai,
    Nippon Mesojisutō Shizuoka Kyōkai rokujūnen shi (Shizuoka: Nippon Mesojisutō Shizu-
    oka Kyōkai, 1936), 39–50. See also Ōta Aito, *Meiji Kirisutokyō no ryūiki: Shizuoka
    bando to bakushintachi* (Tokyo: Tsukiji Shokan, 1979), 128–47; A. Hamish Ion, *The
    Cross and the Rising Sun: The Canadian Protestant Missionary Movement in the Japanese
    Empire, 1872–1931* (Waterloo, Ontario: Wilfrid Laurier University Press, 1990), 41–
    50. Also of interest is A. Hamish Ion, "Edward Warren Clark and the Formation of
    the Shizuoka and Koishikawa Christian Bands (1871–1879)," in *Foreign Employees in
    Nineteenth-Century Japan*, ed. Edward R. Beauchamp and Akira Iriye (Boulder, CO:
    Westview Press, 1990), 171–89. Among other significant members of this second
    Shizuoka Band were Takagi Mizutaro (1864–1921), who became a pastor and later
    president of Aoyama Gakuin; Takagi Nobutake (b. 1872), who became a journalist
    and editor of the *Tokyo nichi nichi shinbun*; Ōta Torakichi (b. 1864), who became a
    pastor in the Japan Methodist Church; and Hisanaga Katsushige, who also became a
    priest. See Nihon Kirisutokyōdan Shizuoka Kyōkai, *Nihon Kirisutokyōdan Shizuoka
    kyōkai hachijūnen shi* (Shizuoka: Nihon Kirisutokyōdan Shizuoka Kyōkai, 1959), 13.

(1836–1905), a Canadian Methodist medical missionary, with converts from the Tokugawa ex-samurai who were his students at the Shizuhatasha school and before that of Edward Warren Clark (1849–1907), an American layman, at the Shizuoka Gakkō. The Shizuoka Methodist Church in 1886 was the second largest church in the Canadian Methodist-supported Japan Methodist Church.[7] Japanese Christians played a key role in the development of English language education in Shizuoka and its surrounding prefecture. Yamaji was initially attracted to the Shizuoka Methodist Church in order to take advantage of English lessons and was drawn to Christianity by Hiraiwa Yoshiyasu (1857–1933), who was then serving as the pastor of the church.[8] Hiraiwa was already known to Yamaji as the author of articles dealing with Yasui Sokken's *Benmō* (Exposition of Error), which were published in the Christian journal *Rikugō zasshi*.[9] Hiraiwa's reputation was further enhanced because he came to Shizuoka recommended by Naka-

7. In 1886 the Shizuoka Methodist Church had 183 members (88 males, 57 females, and 38 children), and some 82 (62 adults and 20 children) had been baptized that year. The Azabu Methodist Church in Tokyo was the largest church with 213 members. See Yamamoto Yukinori, "Yamaji Aizan to Kirisutokyō: Meiji nijū nendai o chushin to shite," *KSMK* 28 (1977.12): 103–62, 121. Importantly, in Shizuoka Prefecture in addition to the Shizuoka Methodist Church there was also the smaller Numazu Methodist Church. It had come into being in 1877 through the efforts of George Meacham, the Canadian Methodist missionary teacher at the Numazu Chu Gakkō, with the encouragement of Ebara Soroku (1842–1922), the school headmaster who would, in later life, become the leading lay member of the Japan Methodist Church. See Ebara Sensei Den Hensan Iinkai, *Ebara Soroku sensei den* (Tokyo: Ebara Sensei Den Hensan Iinkai, 1924), 203–17. During the mid-1880s Ebara was active as a lay preacher and was a figure who commanded respect among former Tokugawa adherents in part because of his heroism in the Restoration wars. There were close relations between the Shizuoka and Numazu Christian groups, especially in their rural evangelistic efforts.
8. For a history of early English-language education in Shizuoka Prefecture, see Iida Hiroshi, *Shizuoka ken eigaku shi* (Tokyo: Kōdansha, 1967). For Hiraiwa Yoshiyasu, see Kuranaga Takashi, *Hiraiwa Yoshiyasu den* (Tokyo: Kyōbunkan, 1938).
9. See Yamamoto Yukinori, "Rikugō zasshi to Hiraiwa Yoshiyasu," in *Rikugō zasshi no kenkyū*, ed. Dōshisha Daigaku Jinbun Kagaku Kenkyūjo Hen (Tokyo: Kyōbunkan, 1984), 1:233–57. See also Sakamoto Takao, *Yamaji Aizan* (Tokyo: Yoshikawa Kōbunkan, 1988), 36–37; Yamamoto Yukinori, "Yasui Sokken no *Benmō* to Meiji shonen no Kirisutokyōkai," *KSMK* 32 (1984.3): 68–128. For an early English translation of *Benmō* see Yasui Chuihei, *Benmō or An Exposition of Error: being a treatise against Christianity, with a Preface by Shimazu Saburo*, trans. J. H. Gubbins (Yokohama: Japan Mail, 1875).

mura Masanao (1832–91).[10] In 1887 Kobayashi Kōtai (1858–99) replaced Hiraiwa as the pastor of the Shizuoka Methodist Church and clearly inspired the young members of the church both in terms of their English studies and literary activities;[11] he also stimulated their interest in evangelistic work.[12] In early 1888 Yamaji's intimate involvement with the Shizuoka Methodist Church was illustrated by the fact that his name was among the five stewards of that church who informed George Cochran, the chairman of the Japan District of the Methodist Church of Canada, that the Shizuoka Methodist Church had grown sufficiently to become self-supporting.[13] Later in the same year, on Hiraiwa's re-commendation, Yamaji entered the Canadian Methodist mission school, the Tōyō Eiwa Gakkō, in Azabu, Tokyo. Graduating from the mission school in 1890, Yamaji began evangelistic work in Fukuroi in Shizuoka Prefecture for the Japan Methodist Church, but as it turned out he entered Christian journalism rather than becoming a clergyman like his Shizuoka friends, Takagi Mizutarō or Ōta Torakichi, who had also gone up to the Tōyō Eiwa Gakkō at the same time as he had. It needs to be pointed out that Japanese

10. For a useful biography of Nakamura Masanao (Keiu), see Takahashi Masao, *Nakamura Keiu* (Tokyo: Yoshikawa Hiroshi Bunkan, 1967). For a study of Nakamura Masanao and Christianity and, in particular, of his authorship in 1871 of *Gi taiseijin jōsho* (An Imitation of a Westerner's Memorial), in which he advocates the adoption of Christianity by the emperor and the Japanese people, see Osawa Saburo, "Nakamura Keiu to Kirisutokyō: 'Gi Taiseijiin Jōsho' no Chosha," chap. 8 in *Nihon Purotesutanto shi kenkyū* (Tokyo: Tōkai Daigaku Shuppankai, 1964), 228–49. For Nakamura's recommendation of Hiraiwa, see Yamamoto, "Yamaji Aizan to Kirisutokyō," 108. For a study of Nakamura and the Japanese Enlightenment, see Ogihara Takashi, *Nakamura Keiu to Meiji keimō shisō* (Tokyo: Waseda Daigaku Shuppansha, 1984). During the 1880s Nakamura became interested, as Yamaji did later on, in Unitarianism and moved away from the orthodox Christianity of the Japan Methodist Church. However, Nakamura remained on friendly terms with George Cochran until his death.

11. Yamamoto, "Yamaji Aizan to Kirisutokyō," 111.

12. Francis A. Cassidy, who was the Canadian Methodist missionary in Shizuoka from 1886 to 1893, was also very actively involved in teaching English. Miss M. J. Cunningham, a missionary of the Canadian Methodist Woman's Missionary Society, was also involved in teaching; she came to Shizuoka in 1887 to become the first headmistress of the Canadian Methodist school for girls, the Shizuoka Eiwa Jo Gakkō. See Iida, *Shizuoka ken eigaku shi*, 50–51. See also Shizuoka Eiwa Jo Gakuin Hachijūnen Shi Hensan Iinkai, *Shizuoka Eiwa Jo Gakuin hachijūnen shi* (Shizuoka: Shizuoka Eiwa Jo Gakuin, 1971), 29–38.

13. Shizuoka Eiwa Jo Gakuin Hachijūnen Shi Hensan Iinkai, *Shizuoka Eiwa Jo Gakuin hachijūnen shi*, 118–19.

evangelists and pastors in the Japan Methodist Church were extremely poorly paid, and it was particularly difficult for married pastors to make ends meet. Yamaji's opportunity to move into Christian journalism came in 1891 when it was decided that the Canadian Methodist mission should join with the two American Methodist Episcopal missions to create a united Methodist journal, *Gokyō*, and Hiraiwa recommended Yamaji as a suitable editor.[14]

At the time that Yamaji became the editor of *Gokyō*, the Japan Methodist Church in Tokyo was going through a dynamic period of expansion centered on the newly built Central Tabernacle Church associated with the Canadian Methodist missionary, Charles Eby (1845–1925), who deeply influenced many of the younger Japanese members of the church with his evangelistic fire and dynamic lectures.[15] At the end of 1892 Yamaji obviously felt secure enough to marry Tajima Taneko, a Christian graduate of the Canadian Methodist girls' school in Tokyo, the Tōyō Eiwa Jo Gakkō.[16] However, the buoyant evangelistic climate within the Japan Methodist Church changed in 1894 when Charles Eby returned home on furlough to Canada to face charges brought against him by missionaries from the Canadian Methodist Woman's Missionary Society. This led to the premature end of his career as a Japan missionary. The fall of Eby and also of his close friend, Francis Cassidy, soon to be followed by the retirement of George Cochran, one of the most revered Canadian Methodist pioneer missionaries, ushered in a period of both financial retrenchment and theological conservatism for the Japan Methodist Church.[17] Unfortunately, Yamaji was associated with the Eby camp, that is, the

---

14. Kawasaki, "Tōkoku, Aizan, Meiseki, Kandō," 155. It was the intention to create in *Gokyō* a journal that would be of the same standard as Kozaki Hiromichi's and Yokoi Tokio's *Kirisutokyō shinbun* and Uemura Masahisa's *Fukuin shuhō*. It also should be stressed that literary work was an important facet of church activity at the Shizuoka Methodist Church.

15. During 1891–92 Kitamura Tōkoku had a job helping Eby with Japanese translations, and it is this connection that led to Yamaji being introduced to Kitamura. Hiraiwa Yoshiyasu was another who was greatly influenced by Eby's magnetism and ideas.

16. See Tōyō Eiwa Jo Gakuin Hyakūnen Shi Hensan Jikkō Iinkai, ed., *Tōyō Eiwa Jo Gakuin hyakūnen shi* (Tokyo: Tōyō Eiwa Jo Gakuin Hyakūnen Shi Hensan Jikkō Iinkai, 1984), 151–54.

17. Albert Carman, the long-serving superintendent of the Methodist Church of Canada and Alexander Sutherland, the secretary of the Missionary Society of the Methodist Church of Canada, were theologically conservative and quite prepared to use their

losing side within the politics, both secular and theological, of the Japan Methodist Church. It is not surprising, therefore, that 1895, which was also the year of the Triple Intervention, saw Yamaji moving away from active Christianity. While Yamaji did serve on the Discipline Committee of the Japan Methodist Church during the 1890s, he resigned his position at *Gokyō* in 1897 and moved to Nagano. This did not mark the end of his dealings, however, with either Canadian missionaries or the Japan Methodist Church, for these came to a climax in 1901 with the Prudham case, in which Yamaji charged William Prudham, the resident, married Canadian Methodist missionary in Nagano, with the sexual harassment of a female Japanese servant.[18] Yamaji was, certainly, a nuisance to Canadian Methodist missionaries, and it is highly likely, after the departure of Eby and long before the Prudham case, that the more conservative among them, like Davidson McDonald, no longer considered him a Christian.

In the light of Yamaji's bitter experiences with Canadian Methodist missionaries, it is no surprise to see that missionaries got short shrift in *Essays*. Moreover, while his own early career owed much to the support of missionaries and also to Japan Methodists in Shizuoka and Tokyo, he seemed to have no sense of obligation to them. It is evident that Yamaji held the position that Christianity was from a Jew and had to do with the heart, and was not something necessarily attached to Westernization.[19] If he ap-

---

authority to stop the spread of liberal theological ideas within the Canadian Methodist Church, including its Japan Conference. Alexander Sutherland personally disliked Eby because he thought him a spendthrift. For the so-called "Japan Affair," which led to the cashiering of both Eby and his friend Cassidy, see Rosemary R. Gagan, *A Sensitive Independence: Canadian Methodist Women Missionaries in Canada and the Orient, 1881–1925* (Montreal: McGill-Queen's University Press, 1992), 92–95.

18. Shiori, "Nagano jidai no Yamaji Aizan," 181. Even though the Canadian Methodist authorities in Toronto were not prepared to accept the validity of Yamaji's charges, Prudham returned to Canada with his career ruined. Importantly, for the future of Canadian-Japanese relations, Prudham's missionary replacement in Nagano was Dan Norman, whose son, Egerton Herbert, was born in Nagano, and would go on to become the most famous of Canadian Japanologists. The Prudham case marked the end of Yamaji's contact with Canadian missionaries and with the Japan Methodist Church.

19. Author's notes on paper given by Yamamoto Yukinori on Yamaji Aizan in Professor Sugii Mutsurō's Kenkyūkai on Japanese Christianity at the Jinbun Kagaku Kenkyūjo Dōshisha University, Kyoto, Japan, May 10, 1979.

pears rather critical in *Essays*, his criticisms were against Christians rather than Christianity. Clearly, Yamaji's use of his own experiences and background is very selective. His neglect of the role of missionaries in the development Meiji Protestantism has undoubtedly contributed to the fact that Japanese historians, until recently, have portrayed Meiji Christian history largely in terms of the Japanese acceptance of Christianity and have failed to pay sufficient attention to Western missionaries who communicated the new ideas to the Japanese. Another reason the complexity of the reciprocal influence between missionaries and the Japanese has been underestimated, as far as Western academic writing on Japan is concerned, is that unlike China, where the emphasis is on missions and missionaries as well as on converts, in Japan the concern has largely until recently been on the convert rather the missions.[20] This reflected the prime concern, since the 1960s, of Western historians of Bakumatsu and Meiji Japan with the modernization of Japan during the late nineteenth and early twentieth centuries. Christianity was seen as important only in so far as its ideas or individual Japanese Christians played a role in Japan's modernization.[21] This fits in nicely with Yamaji's argument that Protestantism was an important factor in the transformation of Japanese society. If, indeed, missionaries are included, as was the case in John Howes' influential article on American missionaries and Japanese Christians, Meiji Protestantism is seen mainly in terms of the transference of American Puritanism largely from New England roots to Japan and its adaption to the Japanese setting by outstanding Japanese Christian leaders.[22] Such a position does not

20. In part the emphasis on missionaries in China was indicative of the influence of John King Fairbank, the Harvard sinologist, who pointed out the importance of missionary archival materials as a source of information about American and Western activities in China. There was also an apologetic concern in the United States to show, in reappraising Sino-American relations in the wake of the debacle of the American Vietnamese War, that even though the American Protestant missionary movement was a part of the Western imperialism in China before 1951, its influence, particularly in the foundation of Christian schools and colleges, was not entirely harmful.

21. This is seen in Irwin Scheiner's classic study of Japanese Christian protest in Meiji Japan. See Irwin Scheiner, *Christian Converts and Social Protest in Meiji Japan* (Berkeley and Los Angeles: University of California Press, 1970).

22. This is clearly seen in John F. Howes, "Japanese Christians and American Missionaries," in *Changing Japanese Attitudes Toward Modernization*, ed. Marius B. Jansen (Princeton: Princeton University Press, 1965), 337–68. esp. 340–42.

fully take into account the diversity of Protestant Christian ideas (including those of non-Calvinist denominations such as the Methodists or Anglicans) that entered Japan after 1859.

One of the most famous of Yamaji's assertions concerning the acceptance of Christianity in Meiji Japan was that samurai from the losing side in the Restoration turned to Christianity largely in an effort to regain lost status.[23] This was an argument that Irwin Scheiner used in *Christian Converts and Social Protest in Meiji Japan*, which was published in 1970.[24] Indeed, there are few studies of Meiji Protestantism that do not make reference to Yamaji's deracinated samurai argument.[25] To support his opinion, Yamaji used the example of the conversion of the members of the earliest of Protestant groups, the so-called Yokohama Band, formed in 1872.[26] The importance of this particular Christian band was further underlined in the collection of materials, much of it dealing with Japanese Christian history, surrounding the life and times of Uemura Masahisa (1858–1925), the famous Presbyterian who was a member of the Yokohama Band.[27] However, Christian conversion was not restricted to those of the samurai class, for there were also many other converts who were not samurai, particularly in rural areas. While Christian ideas were introduced into Japan through Chinese-language sources as well as through English-language and Western studies, the desire to acquire new knowledge to equip themselves better to changing times was common to most converts regardless of class. The attraction of Christianity was different to people of different classes. While some of the ex-samurai hoped that they could serve their country through their com-

---

23. Yamaji Aizan, "Gendai Nihon kyōkai shiron," in *Kitamura Tōhoku, Yamaji Aizan shū, Gendai Nihon bungaku taikei* 6 (Tokyo: Chikuma Shobō, 1969), 223–71, 230.

24. Scheiner, *Christian Converts*, 22–25, esp. 22–23. The recent Japanese interest in local Christian history largely began after Scheiner's research was completed. In that sense, *Christian Converts* now is dated, and some of Scheiner's conclusions can be challenged on the basis of new and broader evidence.

25. See, for instance, Sugii Mutsurō, *Meiji shoki Kirisutokyō no kenkyū* (Kyoto: Dōshisha Shuppan, 1984), 25; Dohi, *Nihon Purotesutanto Kirisutokyō shi*, 43.

26. For a brief study of the formation of the Yokohama Band, see Dohi Akio, "Nihon saisho no Purotesutanto kyōkai," *KSMK* 8 (1964.4): 24–33.

27. Saba Wataru, ed., *Uemura Masahisa to sono jidai*, 8 vols. (Tokyo: Kyōbunkan, 1937–41). This collection remains an important source of information on the history of the Japanese Christian movement.

mitment to Christianity, "wealthy farmers and merchants . . . found in Christianity a new religio-ethical concept that emphasized the equality of all humanity, created by God and redeemed by Jesus Christ."[28] In the country villages, family relations, family influence, and economic power could prove to be powerful incentives to cause villagers to become Christians, as was illustrated in the case of Shimosa Fukuda near Narita in Chiba Prefecture north of Tokyo, which became an important Anglican stronghold in the years after 1877.[29] There was a very considerable diversity in the way in which different groups accepted Christianity, which Yamaji chose to ignore. In contradiction to his own argument that it was ex-Tokugawa samurai who were attracted to Christianity, Yamaji brought up the Kumamoto Band, which was made up of young men who did not belong to the losing side in the Restoration Wars.[30]

It is from the Kumamoto Band, formed in 1876, that many of the future leaders of the Kumiai (Congregationalist) Church came. Although Yamaji's friend, Tokutomi Sohō (1863–1957), might have played down the fact in later life, Tokutomi himself had signed the Mount Hanaoka Oath, which served as the charter for the Kumamoto Band, and, together with other band members such as Kozaki Hiromichi and Ebina Danjō (1856–1937), had come to Dōshisha College in Kyoto.[31] While Tokutomi put his Chris-

28. Dohi Akio, "Christianity in Japan," in *Christianity in Asia, 1: North East Asia*, ed. T. K. Thomas (Singapore: Christian Conference of Asia, 1979): 35–66, 41.

29. See Nishiyama Shigeru, "Shimosa Fukuda seikokai no keisei to tenkai (jo)," *Shingaku no koe* 18.2 (1972.6): 10–27; Nishiyama Shigeru, "Shimosa Fukuda seikokai no keisei to tenkai (shita)," *Shingaku no koe* 19.2 (1973.6): 21–39.

30. There is considerable literature on the Kumamoto Band. Of particular interest is the work of members of the Kirisutokyō Shakai Mondai Kenkyūjo at the Jinbun Kagaku Kenkyūjo of Dōshisha University in Kyoto as seen in the special issue of their journal on Kumamoto Band research: *Kumamoto Bando no kenkyū tokushū*, KSMK 7 (1963.4). In English, there is Fred G. Notehelfer, "Leroy Lansing Janes and the American Board," in *Nihon no kindaika to Kirisutokyō*, ed. Dōshisha Daigaku Jinbun Kagaku Kenkyūjo Kirisutokyō Shakai Mondai Kenkyūkai (Tokyo: Shinkyō Shuppansha, 1973), 3–5, as well as Notehelfer's superlative biography of Janes, *American Samurai: Captain L. L. Janes and Japan* (Princeton: Princeton University Press, 1985). See also Kozaki Hiromichi, *Reminiscences of Seventy Years: The Autobiography of a Japanese Pastor*, trans. Kozaki Nariaki (Tokyo: Christian Literature Society of Japan, Kyo Bun Kwan, 1934); Kozaki Hiromichi, *Nanajūnen no Kaiko* (Tokyo: Kaiseibo Shashoten, 1928).

31. John D. Pierson, *Tokutomi Sohō 1863–1957: A Journalist for Modern Japan* (Princeton: Princeton University Press, 1980), 52–53. See also Sugii Mutsuro, "Tokutomi Sohō

tianity into abeyance after leaving Dōshisha in 1880,[32] Yamaji, for the purposes of *Essays*, considered Tokutomi a Christian during the 1880s. The fact that Niijima Jō (1843–90), the leading Japanese Christian figure at Dōshisha College and the man who had baptized Tokutomi, should agree to write a forward to the third edition of Tokutomi's *The Future Japan*, in February 1887,[33] is another indication that, at that date, Tokutomi was still regarded by his Christian friends as one of them. Indeed, whatever Tokutomi might later claim, Yamaji argues that the success of Tokutomi Sohō's journal, *Kokumin no tomo*, and also that of Iwamoto Yoshiharu's magazine, *Jogaku zasshi*, during the late 1880s was "proof that Christianity was looked on with favor by the world."[34] Part of the reason Christianity had an important impact on the intellectual world of Meiji Japan was that a considerable number of young Japanese intellectuals were influenced by it at one stage or another in their intellectual development.[35] In that sense, the wider the net is cast among Christian apostates, the greater the influence that can be attributed to Christianity on the intellectual life of Meiji Japan.

Tokutomi was very young when the Kumamoto Band was formed. It was one of the older members, Kozaki Hiromichi (1856–1938),[36] who gave a reason for their Christian conversion by stating that band members "embraced Christianity, because we be-

---

ni okeru Kirisutokyō," *KSMK* 18 (1971.3): 27–99, esp. 31–35. For a brief article on the impact of the Kumamoto Band on the development of literature at Dōshisha, see Sugii Mutsurō, "Kumamoto Bando. Dōshisha to bungaku: 'Dōshisha bungaku' no taido" *Bungaku* 47.4 (1979), 167–86. The importance of Meiji Christianity to literature in Japan is underlined by the fact that two issues of *Bungaku* 47.3 and 47.4, both published in 1979, are entirely devoted to the essays dealing with that subject.

32. Pierson, *Tokutomi Sohō 1863–1957*, 53.

33. See Tokutomi Sohō, *The Future Japan*, trans. and ed. Vinh Sinh, Matsuzawa Hiroaki, and Nicholas Wickenden (Edmonton: University of Alberta Press, 1989), 11–12.

34. See below, p. 138. Yamaji, "Gendai Nihon kyōkai shiron," 254.

35. For a recent article dealing with the impact of Christianity on the Japanese literary world, see Mark Williams, "From out of the Depths: The Japanese Literary Response to Christianity," in *Japan and Christianity: Impacts and Responses*, ed. John Breen and Mark Williams (Basingstoke: Macmillan, 1996), 156–74.

36. For a brief study of Kozaki Hiromichi's thought and actions, see Dohi Akio, "Kozaki Hiromichi: shisō to kōdō," *KSMK* 16/17 (1970.3): 1–37.

lieved that it fulfills the spirit and real import of Confucianism."[37]
Fred G. Notehelfer has pointed out that members of the Kumamoto Band did not suffer from a sense of loss of position and status, which, Irwin Scheiner has suggested, drawing on Yamaji's argument, drove those samurai from the losing side in the Restoration to try to regain their lost position and status through conversion to Christianity. Instead, they apparently felt "an extreme
sense of moral dislocation," which was rooted in the breakdown
of the traditional value system.[38] Christian ethics as taught by
Captain Janes at the Yōgakkō School in Kumamoto, Professor
Notehelfer has argued, helped them not only "to deal with their
sense of moral dislocation, but suggested new possibilities for a
moral and ethical restructuring that maintained the strong public,
or political, commitment that had been part of the Confucian ethical structure in which they had been socialized."[39]

In the cases of Yokoi Tokoi (1857–1927) and Ebina Danjō,
two of the most prominent members of the Kumamoto Band, their
acceptance of Christian ideas was made easier because they could
link them to Confucian concepts, particularly those of the hetero-
doxical Wang Yang-ming (Ōyōmei).[40] In *Essays*, Yamaji points to
Nakamura Masanao, one of the leading Japanese Confucian scholars of his generation, explaining Christianity from the perspective of Confucianism. Dohi Akio has argued that "Christianity as
the fulfillment of what the Japanese culture had been seeking"
was one Japanese response to the Christian faith.[41] Confucianism
prepared the way for early converts like Kozaki to accept Chris-

---

37. See Kozaki, *Reminiscences of Seventy Years,* 39. Fred. G. Notehelfer has stressed Kozaki's
    view of the importance of conversion to Christianity as a fulfilment of Confucian-
    ism. See Notehelfer, *American Samurai,* 205. Of special interest concerning Kozaki
    Hiromichi and Confucianism is Helen Ballhatchet, "Confucianism and Christianity
    in Meiji Japan: The Case of Kozaki Hiromichi," *Journal of the Royal Asiatic Society* 2
    (1988): 349–69.
38. Notehelfer, *American Samurai,* 187.
39. Ibid.
40. Ibid., 188, 329n.9. Dohi Akio stressed the importance of Chinese-language Christian
    books in helping to convey Christian ideas to the Japanese as well as the concepts
    of heaven and of a supreme being that intellectuals of samurai background, particu-
    larly those with a grounding in revivalist forms of neo-Confucianism or Ōyōmei,
    could relate to Confucianism. See Dohi, *Purotesutanto Kirisutokyō shi,* 48.
41. Dohi, "Christianity in Japan," 42.

tianity, and Christianity in its turn served to perfect Confucian values. Yamaji's emphasis on Christianity and Confucianism was part of his attempt to demonstrate the importance of the role of Protestantism in helping to transform traditional Japanese culture. The linkage of Christianity to Confucianism can also be seen as one reason for the early growth of Christianity. It is more debatable whether or not the breakdown of Confucian influence (with its ethical emphasis) on Japanese society was a reason for the later decline of Christianity. While Ōyōmei or other forms of Confucianism did help early on in the conversion of some samurai, it is plain that the understanding of Christianity of these converts also quickly evolved beyond the ethical basis that their Confucian background could relate to.

Further, as Yamaji does indicate, the efforts of Japanese Christian leaders in the 1880s and 1890s were directed to making the Christian message relevant to the intellectual trends (be they evolutionary theories, new Christian theology, or the connection between the concept of the development of the modern self and Christianity) within the changing intellectual world of Japanese society. Christian leaders were also attempting to meet the challenges posed by government to freedom of thought in education occurring at that time. Indeed, it was the failure of the conservative wing of the Protestant movement to keep up with the new liberal theological trends that seemingly draws so much of Yamaji's ire.

On occasion, however, other different traditional values in Japanese culture (substitutes for Confucianism, more in keeping with the changing times) were linked to Christianity. Uemura Masahisa, the leading pastor in the Japanese Presbyterian Church at the time, saw in the aftermath of the Russo-Japanese War the perfection of Bushido, the code of the samurai, by Christianity as a means of helping to transform Japanese culture.[42] (There was in this perhaps an element of nostalgia on the part of aging Christian leaders for the simpler ethical values of their youth.) Imai Judo (Toshimichi, 1863–1919), the leading Anglican clergyman of his

---

42. Ibid.

generation, saw Yamato Damashii (Japanese spirit) as the special characteristic of Japan that could be perfected by Christianity.[43] While Japanese Christians attempted to graft Christianity onto a Japanese root, Western Christian forms of worship introduced into Japan could also sometimes serve to reinforce Japanese values. This was seen, for instance, in the Japanese Anglican prayers for the Meiji emperor.[44] Over the course of time the impact of such prayers perhaps helped to make Japanese Anglicans more sympathetic than other Christians to *tennosei*.

As Japanese Christians were attempting to accommodate their religion to Japanese culture, they were confronted by the challenge of evolutionary theory imported from the West and championed by Katō Hiroyuki and others at Tokyo Imperial University. In *Essays*, Yamaji commends both the way in which Japanese Christians at Dōshisha and other Christian schools as well as those in Tokyo rallied to combat the danger to Christianity from the theory of evolution, and the significant role played by the Christian journal *Rikugō zasshi*. However, he apparently underestimated the ability of the Japanese Christians not only to overcome the challenge of evolution but also to use it to support their belief that Christianity was essential to continued Japanese development by arguing that the evolution of religion must keep pace with that of technology. Helen Ballhatchet has argued that the theory of evolution enabled Japanese Christians "to see Japan's non-Christian religions in a constructive way, as an evolutionary preparation for the Japanese for Christianity, and for a Christianity which, in its Japanese form, might well be spiritually superior to that of the materialistic West."[45] Already, by the end of the Meiji era, the desire for an independent Christianity in Japan had begun to develop signs of the creation of a Japanese Christianity

---

43. Tsukada Osamu, *Shoki Nippon seikōkai no keisei to Imai Judō* (Tokyo: Seikokai Shuppan, 1992), 82–84.

44. See Tsukada Osamu, "Nippon seikōkai kitō sho ni okeru 'Tennō no tame' no sho kitō no keifu," *Kirisutokyō* 25 (1983): 69–92.

45. Helen Ballhatchet, "The Religion of the West versus the Science of the West: The Evolution Controversy in Late Nineteenth Century Japan," in *Japan and Christianity: Impacts and Responses*, ed. John Breen and Mark Williams (Basingstoke: Macmillan, 1996), 107–21, 118.

(Nipponteki Kirisutokyō) distinct from the Christianity propagated by foreign missionaries.

Other than theological and religious arguments[46] against the acceptance of Christianity, the Achilles' heel of Japanese Christians was the doubt that was cast into the minds of non-Christian Japanese about their loyalty to Japan and even their Japaneseness when they became Christians. The specter of Yasui Sokken's *Benmō* and the anti-Christian criticisms of Inoue Tetsujirō that Yamaji tried to counter in *Essays* would continue to haunt the Japanese Christian movement until the end of the Pacific War.

Many Japanese Christian leaders who had emerged out of the Yokohama and Kumamoto Bands outlived Yamaji and continued to dominate the leadership positions in the Japanese Protestant movement until the early 1930s. Although almost all of them had expressed strong nationalist sentiments and striven to reduce the dependence of the Japanese Christian movement on foreign influence and help, nearly all of them had passed away before events leading up to or during hostilities against the Western powers could tarnish their reputations. After the Pacific War, Japanese authors continued to rely on the experiences of Kozaki Hiromichi and Uemura Masahisa, with the addition of those of Uchimura Kanzō, as can be clearly seen in the early writings of Sumiya Mikio on Japanese society and Christianity.[47] Kudō Eiichi, likewise looking at Japanese society and Christianity, stressed the relationship between the acceptance of Christianity among the *shizoku* (descendants of samurai) and Japanese social economic history during the Meiji period.[48]

The turning point in the Japanese writing of their Christian movement, however, came with the publication in 1979 of

---

46. For a highly useful book on Protestant theologies in Japan, see Charles H. Germany, *Protestant Theologies in Modern Japan: A History of Dominant Theological Currents From 1920–1960* (Tokyo: IISR Press, 1965).

47. See, for instance, Sumiya Mikio, *Nihon shakai to Kirisutokyō* (Tokyo: Tokyo Daigaku Shuppankai, 1954); *Nihon no shakai shisō kindaika to Kirisutokyō* (Tokyo: Tokyo Daigaku Shuppankai, 1968).

48. See, for instance, Kudō Eiichi, *Nihon shakai to Purotesutanto dendo—Meiji ki Purotesutanto shi no shakai keizai shi kenkyū* (Tokyo: Nihon Kirisutokyōdan Shuppanbu, 1970); *Nihon Kirisutokyō shakai keizai shi kenkyū: Meiji shoki o chushin toshite* (Tokyo: Shinkyō Shuppansha, 1980).

Ōhama Tetsuya's study on Meiji Christianity, which paid close attention to the emergence of Christian groups in provincial Japan.[49] In the same year, Dōshisha University's Jinbun Kagaku Kenkyūjo produced a study of Christianity on the Matsumoto plain in Nagano Prefecture, with particular reference to the influence of Iguchi Kigenji (1870–1938) and the Kensei Gijuku school.[50] The importance of this regional approach was underlined with Sumiya Mikio's study of Christianity in Gunma Prefecture outside Tokyo during the Meiji period.[51] Continuing research into Christian history at the regional and local levels has enabled historians to appreciate the rich variety of experience in the early development of the Protestant movement in Meiji Japan. Through such research contact between missionaries and Japanese beyond the main metropolitan centers has been better illuminated. Further, there is interest in the women's missionary movement, as illustrated by Kohiyama Rui's sophisticated treatment of American women missionaries in early Meiji Japan, which combines both Western missionary archival materials with Japanese primary sources.[52] More recently, there has been new work done on prewar Christian denominations.[53] Although not dealing directly with Christianity, Ōta Yuzō's study of English and the Japanese should be of great interest to those studying Meiji Protestantism. Ōta analyzes the fluctuations of Japanese interest in English during the Meiji period and finds that the pattern closely mirrors the ebb and flow of interest in Christianity.[54] Indeed, more than Yamaji might have wished to admit, the acceptance of Protestantism in Meiji Japan possibly might have had less to do with Christianity building on

---

49. See Ōhama Tetsuya, *Meiji Kirisutokyō kaishi no kenkyū* (Tokyo: Yoshikawa Kōbunkan, 1979).
50. Dōshisha Daigaku Jinbun Kagaku Kenkyūjo (Kirisutokyō Shakai Mondai Kenkyūkai), *Matsumoto Tairo ni okeru Kirisutokyō: Iguchi Kigenji to Kensei Gijuku* (Kyoto: Domeiya Shuppan, 1979).
51. Sumiya Mikio, *Nihon Purotesutanto shiron* (Tokyo: Shinkyō Shuppansha, 1983).
52. Kohiyama Rui, *Amerika fujin senkyōshi: rainichi no haikei to sono eikyō* (Tokyo: Tokyo Daigaku Shuppankai, 1992).
53. Dōshisha Daigaku Jinbun Kagaku Kenkyūjo, *Nihon Purotesutanto sho kyoha shi no kenkyū* (Tokyo: Kyōbunkan, 1997), and Shiono Kazuo, *Nippon Kumiai Kyōkai shi kenkyū josetsu* (Tokyo: Shinkyō Shuppansha, 1995).
54. Ōta Yuzō, *Eigo to Nihonjin* (Tokyo: Kōdansha, 1995).

the foundations of Confucianism and other traditional values and more with the impact on society of broad trends in Meiji Japan's international relations with the West.

At the same time as research into the Protestant movement in Japan has widened, there has also been considerable Japanese Christian scholarly interest in the links between Japanese Protestantism and the emerging Protestant movement in Yi Korea.[55] The early interest of Japanese Christians in the propagation of the Christian gospel in Korea in the 1880s can be taken as a manifestation of the altruistic desire of many Japanese to help Korea to modernize in the face of the threat of Western imperialism. It was, however, an altruistic desire that, as the Meiji period progressed, came to coincide conveniently with Japan's own imperialistic ambitions in the peninsula. Nationalism with its demands of patriotism led the Japanese Christian movement to be identified as supporting Japan's expansionism overseas especially after the Russo-Japanese War. In their support of Japanese imperial and military ambitions in continental East Asia, Japanese Christians could demonstrate visibly their loyalty to Japan to counter the doubts about their Japaneseness raised by their adherence to a foreign religion identified with the West. Just as academic attention has been paid to the relationship between Christianity and modernization in Meiji Japan, so, too, attention must also be paid to the relationship between Christianity and Japanese overseas expansionism in the years following the Sino-Japanese War of 1894–95. While they were advocates of religious imperialism in the form of a Japanese missionary movement overseas, many Japanese Christians also supported Japanese imperialism and colonialism. In this, of course, the reaction of Christians bore a striking resemblance to that of Japanese Buddhists, who, like Christians, suffered considerable persecution at the hands of the Meiji government.

In *Essays*, Yamaji Aizan was able to show that Japanese Christians were motivated by a deep desire to improve Japan and

55. See, for instance, Kogawa Keiji and Ji Myon Kwan, eds., *Ni Kan Kirisutokyō kankei shiryō 1876–1922* (Tokyo: Shinkyō Shuppansha, 1984).

its society. Moreover, he was able to demonstrate in *Essays*, whatever its detractors might choose to believe, that Christianity was important to the transformation of Japan from a traditional to a modern society.

Essays on the History of the Modern Japanese Church

1

INTRODUCTION

The main reason for the lack of spiritual vitality of the Japanese people was the policy of the Tokugawa. In the Tokugawa period, Buddhism became, more or less, the only state religion. It received the protection of the state. Even if Buddhist priests did not go out and do evangelical work themselves, the people had to be registered with a temple as believers in order to prove they were not members of a heretical sect. To put this in other words, the so-called temple certificates of that time were like the family registers of today. For the good citizen they were things that could not be done without. While remaining seated, Buddhist priests were able to gather believers. While remaining seated, they were able to feed and clothe themselves. This political favor, however, caused the Buddhists to lose their evangelical spirit. It dulled the spirit of the people for studying the Way. Finally, it turned religion into a kind of ceremony.

Yet, in people's hearts there is a spirit. The heart cannot endure emptiness. The Japanese people, seeing temples dozing in the favor of the state, sought the freedom of spiritual activity independently and outside the walls of the temple. For this reason, the ideas of the Zhu Xi school and the Wang Yang-ming school were taught.[1] For this reason, the teachings of Jinsai, Sorai, and

---

1. The Zhu Xi school was the official ideology of the Tokugawa shogunate while the Wang Yang-ming school was regarded as a form of heterodoxy.

the Eclectic school appeared.[2] Nativist scholars like Mabuchi, Norinaga, and Atsutane also preached a kind of doctrine.[3] There was also the rise of the Mito school that sought to join Confucianism with Nativism.[4] These groups, however, did not go beyond the teachings of the gentry. Among the ordinary people, moral philosophers taught a separate creed that combined Confucianism, Buddhism, and Zen.

The existence of these teachings proves that the investigation of basic truth is a fixed requirement of the human heart and the power of the government was completely unable to suppress it. Vegetation, however, cannot attain full growth in the shade. The Edo government, as a principle, did not permit freedom of thought, and this policy had an extremely powerful influence on the thought of the period. The educated classes used religion simply as a cultural tool. It reached the point where they regarded it is a political convenience. The establishment of the so-called Shinto religion demonstrated their best attitude toward religion, but beyond this they had no religious requirements, and they did not wish to have any.

2. Itō Jinsai (1627–1705) was the most important scholar of Confucianism in the Edo period, and his thought inspired the work of another important philosopher, Ogyū Sorai (1668–1728). The Eclectic school (Setchugakuha) was a school of thought that combined nativism, the Zhu Xi school, and the Wang Yang-ming school of thought. Its principal exponents were Inoue Kinga (1732–84), Katayama Kenzan (1730–82), and Hosoi Heishū (1728–1801).

3. Kamo no Mabuchi (1697–1769), Motoori Norinaga (1730–1801), and Hirata Atsutane (1776–1843) were all important figures in *kokugaku* ("Nativism" or "National Learning"). This movement sought to promote the study of a purely Japanese form of literature and thought by detailed study of ancient texts, and by attacking the influence of Buddhism and Confucianism.

4. The origins of the Mito school can be traced back to the early Tokugawa period when Tokugawa Mitsukuni was the lord of Mito domain. The early school was known for the philosophic diversity of its members. The principal achievement of the school was the compilation of the *Dai Nihonshi* (History of Great Japan).

2

THE AWAKENING OF THE JAPANESE PEOPLE I

The great forces of the world, however, broke down the gates of old Japan and the so-called Restoration revolution took place. If you were to think that this revolution was nothing more than the reform of political institutions or a change of government leaders, then this would be only a superficial understanding. The Restoration was a general revolution. It was a fundamental revolution that passed through both the spiritual and material aspects of society, and not a partial revolution that only involved politics or social life.

What evidence do I have to say this? I know this by reading the work of Yasui Sokken.[5] According to *The Collected Works of Yasui Sokken*, in the early Meiji period a friend of Yasui's had a school with about one hundred students. They often enthusiastically spoke of the virtues of republicanism. Although I do not know how many people said this, they claimed that without republicanism there could be no "rich country, strong army." Moreover, according to the diary of Yokoi Shōnan, at the end of the first year of Meiji, Yokoi heatedly argued about the American House of Rep-

---

5. Yasui Sokken (1799–1876) was a Confucian scholar from Obi domain who studied with Shinozaki Shōchiku (1781–1851) in Osaka. He later became a teacher in his domain's school and, later still, taught at the Shōheikō, the shogunate's academy of Confucian studies. He had diverse interests, including astronomy, calendar making, and the West. After the Restoration he devoted himself to writing and produced, among other things, a critique of Christianity entitled *Benmō* (An Exposition of Error).

resentatives with Mori Arinori.[6] He had an interesting discussion about this all night. Yokoi emphasized the need to abolish the custom of hereditary positions and argued that people with suitable ability should occupy appropriate positions. It is also a fact that, at that time, Baron Katō Hiroyuki[7] was an extreme advocate of democracy. Also, in 1869 or 1870, Ueno Kagenori[8] talked openly and at length about the virtues of American republicanism and praised America as a free country in which there was equality between high and low, rich and poor. When the feudal nobility changed its name to the peerage, the hotheaded but cool-tongued Fukuzawa Yukichi sarcastically remarked, "Those who eat cooked rice are called peers, and those who eat uncooked rice are called beggars." The notion that society extended from the emperor and the shogun at the top down to the farmers and townspeople at the bottom was overturned. Compared to the world of yesterday, thought had undergone a fundamental transformation. This was the case to an extreme degree. The Chinese historian Zhao Yi described the change from the era of the *Spring and Autumn Annals* to that of the Ch'ing-Han period as "a great transformation in

6. Yokoi Shōnan (1809–1869) was a teacher and political adviser who rose to prominence in the last decade of the Edo period. Originally from Kumamoto domain, he gained influence with Matsudaira Yoshinaga, the daimyo of Echizen. When Yoshinaga became the acting head of the shogunal government in 1862, Shōnan went to Edo to act as an adviser. He supported reform within the shogunate, closer cooperation with the imperial court, opening Japan to foreign trade, and greater participation by the larger domains in shogunal affairs. Although Shōnan lost influence after 1863, he was honored by the Meiji government with the position of counselor. He was assassinated in 1869. Mori Arinori (1847–89) was sent to England and America by his domain in 1865 but returned in 1868 to join the new government. He was forced to resign in 1869 for proposing the abolition of sword wearing. He returned to government service in 1870 and served as Japan's first representative in Washington. Mori later became minister of education but was assassinated in 1889.
7. Katō Hiroyuki (1836–1916) was one of the most influential political thinkers in the early Meiji period. Before the Restoration he had a strong interest in the West and was the first person in Japan to study German language and philosophy. After the Restoration he was a supporter of democracy and published numerous works advocating personal liberty. As time progressed, however, he became increasingly conservative and strongly opposed the Freedom and Popular Rights movement. He became such a strong supporter of state supremacy that he disavowed his earlier prodemocratic writings.
8. Ueno Kagenori (1844–88) studied English and Dutch in his native Kagoshima before the Restoration, and in the early Meiji period he worked as a senior foreign ministry official and diplomat.

the world." I think this description best suits the history of the Restoration. Indeed, with regard to the intellectual trend of the times, Yasui Sokken was like the Elder Cato. Confronted with this new kind of thought and overcome with fear, Yasui wanted to fight to protect the isolated castle of Confucianism. Somebody seeing all this would think that the Japanese people have the tendency to easily become attached to new theories and to easily become immersed in debate. Perhaps it is so. This is not, however, to think deeply. The policy of the Edo government of obstructing freedom of thought caused the Japanese people to lack any real beliefs. Suddenly, the light of civilization shone in and in a moment there was freedom of thought. They did not know what to do themselves and, without understanding, they wanted to copy foreign culture. They believed that they could quickly build a new Japan and lightly destroyed time-honored political institutions. In this way, the world changed, the world was washed clean, the world glorified new principles. Along with this, the tendency to copy foreign countries flourished day after day.

In 1873, Inoue Kaoru,[9] who always had the ability to see into the dark side of the times, wrote:

> Now there are people in government service who have not set foot on foreign soil and who still have not seen a foreign country. They have read just a little of a translated foreign book or glanced at a photograph, but they have become strangely aroused and wish to fight against foreign countries. Every year the number of people traveling abroad is increasing. When they return, they say England or Holland or America is unsurpassed, comparing the strong points of these countries with us. Of course this includes streets, currency, land reclamation, and trade, as well as the military, scholarship, discussion, law, steam, telegraphs, clothes, and machines. Nothing remains that will not benefit our culture. Nothing escapes, large or small, that they do not wish to possess.

Inoue was speaking only of the bureaucracy, but what goes through all the nerves goes through the whole body. Was there anyone

---

9. Inoue Kaoru (1836–1915) was a politician who had a distinguished career in Meiji Japan, serving as minister of public works, foreign affairs, agriculture and commerce, home affairs, and finance.

among the so-called progressives who did not hate the old things of Japan and who did not love the new ideas from abroad? It was in this period that Kuroda Kiyotaka,[10] the head of the Land Reclamation Department, after hearing the opinion of a certain American, sent Yamakawa (now Marchioness Ōyama), Tsuda, and other girl students to America to study.[11] It was a time when the scholar of French, Ōi Kentarō, translated the *French Legal Code* and the Ministry of Justice published it.[12] It was the period when Montesquieu's *Spirit of the Laws* was translated. It was in this period that young hostesses chatted with guests, interspersing their speech with foreign words. It was the period when, in various different places in the streets of Tokyo, schools of Western studies hung out their signs. Day by day the number of students who earned a living by teaching broken English increased. Fukuzawa Yukichi[13] provided an example of this from a small book entitled *The Teaching of Language*:

> Having consulted with my relatives, I decided to go to Tokyo to study. On the recommendation of Mr. Superficiality, who lived in Worldly Lane, Tokyo, I entered the Famous School of Professor Dishonesty. It was a very prosperous school with 33,333 students. At that time there were two foreign teachers, an Englishman, Mr. Shoemaker, and an American, Mr. Sailor. There were seven or eight Japanese teachers including Mr. Boastful, Mr. Deceit, and Mr. Sycophant. Everyday they conducted classes.

10. Kuroda Kiyotaka (1840–1900) was a politician from Satsuma domain who worked for cooperation between Satsuma and Choshu loyalists before the Meiji Restoration. After the Restoration he became, first, deputy director and then, in 1874, director of the Hokkaido Colonization Office. In this capacity he worked for the development of Hokkaido in order to defend Japan's northern border against Russia and to find employment for members of the former samurai class.
11. Yamakawa Sutematsu (dates unknown) and Tsuda Umeko (1865–1929) were among fifty-four students sent along with the Iwakura Mission in 1871 to study in the United States.
12. Ōi Kentarō (1843–1922) was one of the leading members of the Freedom and Popular Rights movement in the 1870s and 1880s. In 1882 Ōi joined the Liberal Party and was associated with its radical wing, which advocated "direct action" in order to make the government more democratic.
13. Fukuzawa Yukichi (1835–1901) was one of the most influential thinkers and educators in early and mid-Meiji Japan. In addition to publishing a vast number of essays and books, he also established Keiō College, which developed into the present Keiō University.

One cannot help but be moved by the skill with which, through people's names, he satirized the weakness of the times in one sentence.

Fukuzawa Yukichi, Nakamura Masanao, Mori Arinori, Nishi Amane, and others established the Meirokusha and vigorously supported the idea of Westernization.[14] It was a time when Mori Arinori, an extreme advocate of reform, argued, "If Japanese did not contain Chinese words, it could not be used. Things like national laws do not have to be published in Japanese. For this reason, English should be used as a substitute in general education."

I remember at the time I was living in Shizuoka and the head of our household taught me "A, B, C." I was urged to learn "A, B, C" along with the Japanese alphabet "i, ro, ha." The teacher of the so-called temple school where I was first taught to write with a brush also taught me English pronunciation. I also heard stories from Parley's *History of the World*.[15] I carried the *Analects* and *Introduction to English* to my teacher and was taught how to read them.

I remember at that time there was a young teacher living in the neighborhood who taught English. Also in Shizuoka there was a village called Kawabe. In this village, there was a young girl who was the daughter of a samurai. Even though she was a girl she wore a student *haori* coat that was popular then. She walked about carrying Western books. I remember she was a friend of my grandfather. This was in 1874 or 1875. If things were like this in Shizuoka, which was one hundred and twenty miles from Tokyo, I am sure you can imagine the customs of the time.

14. The Meirokusha was a society whose members were among the most influential intellectuals of the early Meiji period. Beginning in the sixth year of the Meiji period, the society held meetings to discuss topical issues and also published a journal, the *Meiroku zasshi*.

15. Peter Parley's *Universal History on the Basis of Geography for the Use of Families and Schools* (1869) was published numerous times in the 1880s and was widely used as a textbook in Japan.

3

THE AWAKENING OF THE JAPANESE PEOPLE II

Of course, the number of people who pursued Western culture in this way were only a tiny minority in terms of the total population. This is not difficult to understand even if you look at Fukuzawa Yukichi's Keiō College, where the majority of the students were the sons of samurai. This small minority believed it would control the fate of Japan, however, and others also believed this. Indeed, these people did control Japan's fate!

It goes without saying that there were many obstacles to the implementation of reform. The Nativist scholars who had contributed to the Restoration regarded reformers as heretics. The scholars of Chinese studies thought that they were misleading the nation through their irresponsible behavior. The general populace, accustomed to the peace and stability of the Tokugawa era, imagined that the country was being administered by witchcraft, after seeing the way the reformers changed the system and changed the laws. There were disturbances in which people carried bamboo spears and straw-mat flags, because it was thought that people's blood was to be taken as a blood tax, and because it was said a new census was taken in order to send young women overseas.

Walking the streets of Tokyo and looking at the sale of books, one saw the *Doctrine of the Mean* exposed on roadside stalls and the *Analects* covered with cobwebs. A large Buddhist book like *Daihannyakyō* did not have the value of a worthless Western book.

This was the scene in Tokyo, but if, in contrast, you traveled to the provinces, you could see some old Confucian scholars glaring out from their retreats waiting for the time of reaction to come. Old men lamented the decline, day by day, of the old customs, and the trend toward laxness, increasing day by day. There were swordsmen who, never having abandoned the techniques of Bushido, lamented their few students becoming weaker by the day.

The so-called advocates of rapid reform could not escape hearing the enemies' voices that surrounded them on all sides. They believed in themselves. They said, "At a time like the present, what other good policy is there apart from transplanting Western culture? Everything Japanese is bad. Everything European and American is good. The only plan for today is to make Japan Western." Emotionally the opposition party could only gnash their teeth in the face of this argument. From a theoretical point of view, however, they had nothing to surpass this argument. The progressive party had the fewer numbers and the conservative party the greater numbers. The smaller party, however, had sole possession of the knowledge and learning necessary for the age. The larger party—although they had doubts about what the smaller party did, and although they were frustrated by their argument—did not know how to deal with the times. They knew that they did not have the secret key to unlock the riddle of the new age. Even though they were resentful, they put their trust in the things the small party did. Putting their faith for a time in the so-called galloping horses of Westernization, there was nothing they could do but look on. In this way the progressive party took the stage in Japan.

It is not surprising that it was at this time that Christianity first raised its head. Yokohama was then the center for students studying English, and it was there that a missionary from the Dutch Reformed Church, James Ballagh,[16] undertook theological work.

---

16. James Ballagh (1832–1920) was an American missionary who arrived in Japan in 1861. A characteristic of the introduction of Protestantism to Japan in the early Meiji period was the formation of "bands" of Japanese converts centered on the activity of foreign missionaries in particular locations. The "Yokohama Band"—which included Oshikawa Masayoshi (1851–1928), Kumono Yushi (1852–1921), Ibuka Kajinosuke (1854–1940), and Uemura Masahisa (1858–1925)—the "Sapporo Band," and the "Kumamoto Band" were among the most important of these groups.

Ballagh was the center for a group of young people studying Christianity. They were the first to become baptized, and it was there that the basis of the later Christian church was established.

Before I talk about this, however, I must relate how, at the time of the Restoration, politics inflicted suffering on those involved in the Christian disturbance in Nagasaki.

The Restoration government defeated the shogunate's army and, seeing that foreign intercourse was unavoidable, proclaimed the Imperial Restoration, and gave up the "expel the barbarian" slogan with which they had attacked the shogunate. Politically they did nothing more than open the ports, because in their hearts they were still advocates of the idea of "expel the barbarian." Their policy was one of harboring evil thoughts but mouthing good words. This became clear in relation to the Christian disturbance in Nagasaki.

I would like to make the situation at this time clear by summarizing a book called *A Posthumous Record of Fresh Blood* produced by a member of the Roman Catholic Church. In this book there is an introduction explaining that, despite the severe prohibition of the shogunate, there existed in the vicinity of Nagasaki a small group who believed in Christianity and who had secretly followed the beliefs of their ancestors. Among these people, those living in Urakami suddenly appeared at the Roman Catholic Church in the foreign compound of Nagasaki on 17 March 1864. Later the Urakami believers aroused the envy of the Buddhists who complained to the governor of Nagasaki. After the introduction, the book relates how the Restoration government dealt with the Christians:

> The Japanese church revived but immediately a serious problem developed. The Buddhist priests became jealous and wished to crush the Christian church as in old times. The Christians, however, did not weaken at all. Their faith became firmer, and, even when somebody died, they would not tell the Buddhist priests nor would they give alms to them. The Buddhist priests became angry and explained to the village headman of Urakami that recently the number of people belonging to a banned heretical sect in the village had increased, and for this reason he should complain to the au-

thorities at the governor's office. In March 1867, the believers were suddenly called to the governor's office. They underwent a thorough investigation and sixty householders were put in jail unjustifiably. In October of the same year, this was repeatedly discussed in various newspapers in a number of Western countries. The papers sharply advised the Japanese government to permit freedom of religion for the Japanese people, but there was no result. On 4 January 1868, however, at the battle of Fushimi, the oppression of the Tokugawa was torn down in a single day and the enemy of the Christian church was destroyed.

Following on from this, there is a report on the persecution of Christians in the diary of the Council of State for April of the same year. In July 1869, 130 believers from Urakami and Nagasaki were arrested and cruelly tortured at the Nagasaki governor's office in order to make them give up their faith. There are reports of believers often being arrested from the areas of Hizen, Ōmura, and Goshima. About four hundred blameless people were put in prison. They were not given enough food and great suffering was seen. Of the 133 believers in the Ōmura jail, 45 had died of starvation within one year. In 1868, in the month of May, there was a report of plans for Christians from various places to be arrested, divided up among thirty-four daimyo, and severely persecuted in order to make them give up their faith. This was not implemented because of the pressure of national affairs. With the return of national stability in the early Meiji period, however, the priests of various Buddhist temples were like devils opposing Christians and wishing to destroy them. They tried any number of devices to have the three-year-old plan implemented, and they petitioned the Council of State a number of times.

On 1 January 1870, thirteen or fourteen ships showing the flags of various daimyo suddenly gathered in Nagasaki harbor. Lord Watanabe of the Council of State came from Tokyo and handed over a notice from the council to Governor Nomura. He was ordered to make the Urakami Christians board the steamboats. Therefore, Governor Nomura immediately dealt with those arrested and, within four days, all the Christians were chained in the ships as ordered. At this time there were scenes of physical suffering that the human eye had not witnessed before. There were scenes of old people unable to walk freely, staggering along and being driven along like prisoners caught by the devil. There were young children in chains, with their mothers crying because they were separated from their mother's breast. Even outsiders seemed to be moved to pity. It was enough to make an idolater with no feeling cry, so the Europeans who are true people walking the same Christian road felt as if spikes had been driven into their chests. They instantly raised their voices in anguish, and tears ran down their cheeks. There were also some people who became angry and clenched their fists and shook their bodies. Heaven also grieved over this and became angry. Suddenly, the sky clouded over and thunder rolled across the sky. There was a feeling that something was about to fall, and people shuddered. This was a warning that causing the suffering of innocent people was contrary to the way of heaven. All the people hid themselves in closed rooms and were fearful. The Christians, however, most reverently, did not move. Everything is through the grace of God. Although there is no limit to suffering in the name of Christ, Christians are blessed. They advanced encouraging one another. They placed around their necks a white cloth that had been purified in a ceremony and that they had received from a priest at the time of their baptism. They advanced while reading the Scriptures. The depth of their faith was a blessing.

Soon after the church in Japan revived, it encountered this problem. Although it was feared that the church would be cruelly destroyed, in fact, through the mysterious will of God, it was not. Our Lord Christ told the disciples that if a barley seed is not put in the ground to rot, it will not send up shoots and seed. In the same way, through the martyrdom of the saints of the old Japanese church, their descendants threw up shoots and these bore seeds according to the will of God. God protects his servants and mysteriously helps them.

Look! With regard to the previous incident, on 2 January 1870, the various foreign consuls in Nagasaki quickly sent Governor Nomura a letter:

> We do not have any connection with the internal affairs of your country. With regard to the people of Urakami who were persecuted because of their religion, however, we cannot bear merely to look on. We would like to give you a word of warning. Have they committed some crime? They are following the teachings of heaven and they are trying to walk along the way of man. Arresting them in this way and persecuting them is contrary to the way of heaven and the way of man. You will be ridiculed by civilized countries and invite their hostility, so we petition you to release them, follow the way of heaven and the way of man, and stabilize the country.

The Western consuls in Yokohama presented this document to the Council of State and requested talks. The British consul, Lord Parkes, was chosen as a representative, and he met Minister Iwakura.

> The religion observed by the people in Urakami is the same religion we observe. To persecute them is to persecute us. This incident, therefore, is tied to international treaties and it may cause a dispute between your country and the various Western countries. We ask you to give this favorable consideration.

The Minister would not accept this:

> No, the people of our country hate Christianity. The politics of our country are fixed in the rights of the descendants of the gods. For this reason we will persecute Christians as much as possible.

He spoke very directly, so the American Consul De Long spoke up from the side:

> In our country, there is freedom of religion and everyone believes in Christianity. If they hear the news that Christians are persecuted in Japan they will become angry and contact between our countries will be cut. Would it not be very regrettable if our cordial relations turn to bitter enmity? Please consider this. We will not warn you again.

The assertion that restricting the freedom of belief was contrary to the principles of heaven displeased the minister. A number of complications were being created in this situation, so Foreign Minister Taku Nobuyoshi and Terajima Munenori calmed both sides down:

> At any rate, the arrested Christians would be divided up and sent off to daimyo in various places. As much as possible they would be treated well. Parents and children, husbands and wives, brothers and sisters would be sent to the same place. The problem would be dealt with one way or the other.

The consuls returned and soon the news was echoing around Europe. It was recorded and discussed in depth in various newspapers, such as the *Cincinnati Telegraph* on 31 August 1871, the French *Paris Newspaper,* and *The Times* in England.

The Japanese daimyo, however, had had the custom of treating Christians as criminals for over two hundred years. The Buddhist priests also gave way to their desires and persecuted them, so the Christians suffered extreme hardship. Pitifully, in order to force them to abandon their faith, parents and children, husbands and wives, were separated and kept in different places. Sleeves were always wet with tears, and beyond that, because of a shortage of food, many people died. Of the sixteen sent to Tsuwano in Isshu, eleven died of hunger. These people were put into a frozen lake in the middle of winter. Greatly weakened and with only a small amount of food, their strength did not revive and finally they died. The two hundred and fifty people sent to Kaga were severely punished. Those of deepest faith had their clothes taken away in midwinter and, wrapped only in straw mats, spent their nights shivering in jail. It would be difficult to exhaust paper and pen describing the hardships they experienced. Not one person abandoned his faith, but there were many who died and attained the joys of heaven. Those sent to Nagato, also to Koriyama in Washu, and Hiroshima in Keishu, and to other places, all underwent various forms of persecution. The fact that none of them lost even a little of their faith and indeed became braver impressed the officials who persecuted them. There were so many persecuting officials who came to understand the principle of the teachings, who were reformed, and who became Christians, that it is difficult to count them. The Church of God in Ise was established by converted persecuting officials. It is well known that it is now very successful.

There was one thing that was especially moving about the Christians who were sent to the various daimyo. Those with deepest faith took advantage of an unguarded moment and escaped from the jail and hurried, day and night, to the Roman Catholic Church in Osaka. There were many who received the sacrament and then returned to their former prisons.

In the diary of a missionary who lived in Osaka, the names and circumstances are written in detail of groups of three or four people who, thinking of the Sabbath, joined together and left jails in Kinai, Shikoku, and Kyushu. People came especially from Kaga, two hundred miles away. They were completely worn out and could not walk freely, so they were advised to rest for a while, take care of themselves, and return, but they did not listen to the advice. The missionaries were impressed by those who came saying, "We took advantage of an unguarded moment and escaped. We would like to return quickly and apologize." After receiving the sacrament, they quickly stood up and returned. This is truly a believer in difficult circumstances. Even compared to the cherished martyrs of old, they need feel no shame.

Through the mysterious faith of its followers, the compassion of God appeared within the Christian church. There was the decree of the Imperial Restoration, and the daimyo were separated from their domains. As a result of Lord Shimazu's memorial, the Buddhist priests, who viewed Christians as their enemies, encountered a life and death struggle and were thrown into a state of extreme distress. They put the problem of Christianity aside for a time. Through entreaties they were able to fend off this law banning Buddhism, but temple land was taken, they were banned from working as teachers, and they lost a lot of public confidence. There were many who experienced hardship in their lives.

Recalling the story in Luke 1:51, Mary's Song, "The power of his arm has scattered the proud," one understands the terror of God's judgment.

Afterward, the Japanese government strengthened its relations with various Western countries. In order to revise the treaties, talented men were selected and sent abroad. At this time a mysterious event occurred like that in ancient times when God added the enemy general Paul to his disciples in Damascus.

The talented men sent abroad by the Japanese government were Minister of the Right Iwakura Tomomi, Counselor Kido Takayoshi, Finance Minister Terajima Munenori, and Works Minister Itō Hirobumi. At first, Iwakura rejected Christianity and he was like an enemy of the church. Basically, however, Iwakura's intellect surpassed that of ordinary people: he was quick to correct injustice and he was like lightning in illuminating right and wrong. He had this kind of personality, so he quickly understood principles. His good name thunders throughout the countries of the world.

On 22 December 1871, the dignitaries of the foreign mission boarded a steamship, left Yokohama in Japan, and crossed to Washington, D.C., in the United States. They made a first-hand inspection of the republican politics of a federal state and also visited famous places of historical and scenic interest. They left the United States at the end of the same year, and after several days they arrived in Europe. Beginning with England, France, and Germany, they expected to travel around various countries in Europe, and their itinerary was settled. Among the various newspapers in the different European countries that printed articles about the arrival of the Japanese dignitaries, however, the argument by the *London Times* was especially forceful:

> The Japanese Minister of the Right who has arrived now
> is the man who refused to listen to the many appeals of

the foreign consuls at the time the Japanese government
arrested and cruelly tortured Christians. Especially, it was
the plan of this minister to arrest more than three thou-
sand Christians in Nagasaki. If this is correct, then the
minister does not know what the truth is. Vainly empha-
sizing his own prejudicial opinion, he misleads himself and
others.

This article appeared in *The Times* and immediately
people became agitated. Even the people of the Protestant
Church who had no connection with Catholicism could not
remain silent. A professor presented a letter to the foreign
minister saying, "Taking advantage of the visit of the Japanese minister, the Foreign Ministry of our country should
speak the truth and remonstrate with the Japanese minister.
We wish to have our brother Christians in Japan freed and to
have the notices banning Christianity that still remain in various places removed."

The House of Commons discussed this issue heatedly
and pressured the Secretary of Foreign Affairs. The French
Parliament, hearing this, also quickly rose. One famous debater was especially indignant, saying, "The persecution of
innocent Christians by the Japanese government is a disser-
vice to humanity. It is sad that civilized countries have to
grieve for Japan. Western politicians, cooperate and admon-
ish the politicians of Japan. You do not need to have scruples
about showing kindness." In Germany too, people exerted
themselves with regard to Japan.

The minister was very intelligent and soon recognized
the truth. He came to regret the three-hundred-year-old error of the Tokugawa. He telegraphed his opinion to the court
from distant Europe and petitioned that the notices banning
Christianity be removed and the imprisoned Christians freed.
The court was pleased and quickly ordered the authorities to
implement his suggestions. In June 1872, the fame of the
minister spread to every country of Europe. He was respected
for quickly resolving the problem with justice and fairness. It
will be recorded in the history of all countries that the minister alone must be praised for this. It will also be a joy for
Japanese people because, with such a wise minister as the
representative of the Japanese people, they will be praised
for their principles and their courage.

I think this was written by a French missionary. The style often
goes to excess, and in some places his imagination runs away. We
cannot doubt, however, that what is recorded is in general true.

The power of the Christian church had developed to a vast extent in the sixteenth century, but it was swept away by the shogunate. To completely destroy all traces, however, is a very difficult thing to do. We can see that after almost two centuries, in 1829, there was a secret group of Christian believers in Kyoto. This is to say nothing of Kyushu, which was called the heartland of Christianity. Near Nagasaki, from the beginning, there have been people who have not changed their faith but transmitted the creed and ceremonies secretly from generation to generation. The power of the shogunate collapsed and the number of foreigners coming to Japan increased, so they quickly proclaimed that they were Christians. The number of Christians was extraordinarily large, and this was a shock to the governor of Nagasaki. In place of the shogunate, the new government soon had the responsibility of dealing with the heretics who had disregarded the national ban and suddenly appeared.

4

The Appeasement Policy of the Restoration Government; The Surprise of Ōkuma Shigenobu and the Beginning of the New Church

In their treatment of Christianity, the politicians of the Restoration government began with great persecution but ended with gentleness. In the beginning they continued the policies of the shogunate and put up notice boards saying:

"The heretical sect of evil Christianity is banned as before."

Foreign consuls complained that the use of the Chinese character "evil" was inappropriate, so this character was removed. The notice was changed from the one article to the following two:

"The previous ban on the Christian sect must be strictly upheld. Evil heretical sects are strictly forbidden."

This was merely a change of words, and they still maintained the national ban on Christianity. There was, however, the problem of the Christians in Urakami. At first a retainer from Ōmura domain was sent to Nagasaki; the Christians were arrested, and the ban was severely enforced. The Privy Counselor Kido Takayoshi[17] was sent to Nagasaki, and the 3,700 people who had been arrested were distributed throughout various domains. This was done to persuade them to change their beliefs, but they were not frightened of punishments. Not only did none of them succumb to persuasion, but this act brought a very sharp objection

---

17. Kido Takayoshi (1833–77) was one of the major figures in bringing about the alliance between Choshu and Satsuma domains that led to the downfall of the Tokugawa shogunate. His initiatives between 1868 and 1871 as a Meiji government official worked to transform Japan from a feudal society to a centralized, bureaucratic state.

from the French consul and others. It was at this point that the government, which had been conscientiously suppressing Christianity, changed its policy. The religious prisoners were given amnesty and permitted to return to their villages. They were also given an allowance to repair their houses and their fields.

In other words, the Restoration government had begun as an obstacle to Christianity, but within three years it had changed its original objective and adopted a policy of appeasement. In this way, the Christian disturbance in Nagasaki burnt like a straw fire and died out like one.

This incident was, however, a practical lesson that inspired boldness on the part of the foreign missionaries. They had long been waiting and preparing for a good opportunity for missionary work in Japan. From this incident they knew that the thinking of the Japanese government was not unbending. From this incident they could see that Christianity was a problem that caught the attention of the Japanese people. From this incident they could understand that freedom of religion was an objective that might not be difficult to achieve. From this they could confirm that the Japanese people had the moral spirit necessary to produce martyrs. In reality, this incident proved that the moral character of the Japanese people was different from that of other East Asian people.

Ōkuma Shigenobu,[18] who was involved in this incident as a government official, wrote:

> The authority of the government confronted twenty-eight weak young girls and severely commanded them to abandon their beliefs. Asking themselves what transgressions they had committed, they appeared to be very weak but mysteriously refused to move. In anger at the obstinate refusal of the women to fear their superiors, officials applied greater duress, but the Christians became more resolute. From this I discovered that it is difficult to change religious belief through political power.

18. Ōkuma Shigenobu (1838–1922) was one of the major figures of the Meiji political world. He was a political party leader who was twice prime minister and several times a cabinet minister. He also founded Waseda University.

The twenty-eight women did not fear the authority of the law courts; they did not think of the censure of the government; and even death did not make them change their beliefs. This incident demonstrated the moral character of the Japanese people. The foreign missionaries seeing this must surely have felt a sense of gratitude. Feeling that an opportunity had finally come, they enthusiastically began evangelical work.

The missionaries worked as language teachers, and the young people who came to their homes by day and night were filled with the vigor of the spiritual revolution of the time. They saw attempts to sweep away all the old things in society. They saw the very bold ideas advocated by their elders. Could they give up without seizing this new religion? Finally, they confessed their faith. In other words, they were caught in the net the foreign missionaries prepared for the purpose.

It was about this time that the first Christian church was established in Japan in Yokohama. This was about the time that Iwakura Tomomi, in response to the severe attack from public opinion in the West, sent a telegram to the government to have the notices banning Christianity removed.[19]

On 10 March 1872, a committee of eleven established the first Christian church at Yokohama on the waterfront in the foreign compound. The names of the people on the committee were the names of the people who would support the Christian movement in the future. Oshikawa Masayoshi and Kumono Yushi were among the founding eleven members, and Honda Yōichi joined in May. Ibuka Kajinosuke and Uemura Masahisa also joined that year. With the passage of time, these people have become the elders of the church, but at that time they were pink-cheeked youngsters with years ahead of them. They had the resolve to advance onto the spiritual battlefield because their young blood

19. Iwakura Tomomi (1825–83) was one of the few major figures involved in bringing about the Meiji Restoration who was of noble birth. After the Restoration he was appointed to various important positions and was responsible for the formulation of the Charter Oath and the establishment of the prefectural system. In 1871 he headed the Iwakura Mission, a delegation sent to Europe and the United States to observe political and social institutions.

was seething with reformist vigor. Most of them still could not understand English. They still could not read theological books. They read a simple book like *Tendo sogen*,[20] and they had the feeling that they were in contact with something new. They heard lectures in broken Japanese from the enthusiastic Mr. Ballagh and felt as though they were hearing something valuable that they had not heard before. They tasted the sweetness of a new belief that surpassed all the old teachings existing in Japan at that time. They happily became the allies of the new faith.

One of those people was Honda Yōichi.[21] He described his own background:

> In my domain, the Hirosaki domain of the Tsugaru family, it was established that people should study the thought of Zhu Xi. I was not, however, content with this. Above all, the re-fined philosophy of Zhu Xi's cosmology did not suit me. I did not study that kind of philosophy. It was simply that I was not satisfied with the subtleties of Zhu Xi's thought, which sought to industriously clear away minor details. I borrowed and read books from the school storeroom, which were not very easy for students to get permission to see, such as *The Works of Wang Yang-ming, Denshuroku*, and so on. For the same reason I read Kumazawa Banzan's *Shugi gaisho*.[22] I was happy to find that they were more natural than Wang Yang-ming's interpretation of the thought of Zhu Xi. When I became a Christian, the elders in my domain said, "As we expected, he read the works of Wang Yang-ming and first fell into heretical thought, but then because of this he became a Christian." I had not had any spiritual training. I did not believe in Shinto gods or Buddhist deities and did not worship them. If there was something I worshiped in a religious way at that time, it was merely the mausoleum of Lord Tsugaru Masanobu, the

20. *Tendo sogen* (The Final Cause of the Universe) was an introductory work to Christianity written in Chinese by the missionary W. A. P. Martin. It aimed at explaining Christianity using Confucian terminology.

21. Honda Yōichi (1848–1912) was from Hirosaki in Mutsu domain (now Aomori Prefecture). He went to study English in Yokohama in 1870, and it was here that he first came in contact with Christianity. He was baptized in 1872 and went on to become an influential educator and the first bishop in the Japanese Methodist Church.

22. Kumazawa Banzan (1619–91) was an important Confucian thinker of the Edo period. He studied with Nakae Tōju (1608–48), the founder of the Wang Yang-ming school of idealist thought in Japan. The *Shugi gaisho* was a work concerned with social problems and politics.

wise ruler of our domain. Masanobu was the third wise ruler of our domain, and his mausoleum was at Iwakisan about seven miles from Hirosaki. I knelt in front of the mausoleum with feelings of awe and respect.

This is the history of only one person. His spiritual experience, however, resembled that of other young people who joined the church at the time. From seeing the experience of one person, you can imagine that of others.

There are many anecdotes about the early church. For example, at the time of the Nagasaki disturbance there was one believer who was arrested along with the others. At the time of the release order, however, he was accidentally left behind, groaning in chains. A certain person in the Ministry of Justice who was a believer read his name in an old register that was in the ministry and discovered that he was still in prison. That person asked a Western missionary to negotiate with the government, and the man was finally released. If you heard this story today, you could hardly believe it. At the time, however, there was this kind of careless treatment.

In another example, there was a certain person employed as a steward in the church, and he claimed to have fled from Nagasaki. There was no complaint about his behavior as a believer for he often read the Bible and attended all the meetings. There was no point on which to criticize him, but it was simply that nobody knew anything of his family or his village because nobody knew where he had come from. His real character, however, soon became apparent. He was a spy sent by the Buddhists to find out the secrets of the church, and so he had dressed himself up as a believer. Later, he again donned a Buddhist stole and became the head priest of a temple.

5

A Spiritual Revolution Comes from the Dark Side of the Age

I do not want to spend too much time in idle gossip, and thus I will proceed to the essential points. In the beginning, the church consisted mostly of young people. It is common that among those who are old there are few who have the boldness necessary to embrace a new faith. If you were to believe, however, that all types of young people were moved by the new creed, then you would be overlooking an important characteristic of those involved. Let us try to examine the background of those who accepted the new faith.

Was not Uemura Masahisa the son of a shogunate retainer? He experienced the bitterness of defeat common to all the retainers of the shogunate. Honda Yōichi was the child of a Tsugaru man. A person who knows the position of Tsugaru at the time of the Restoration and the hardship there could not doubt that he was a person whose circumstances had been unfavorable. Ibuka Kajinosuke was the son of a person from Aizu. He suffered adversity in which "the country was destroyed, leaving only the mountains and rivers." Oshikawa Masayoshi was the child of a person from Matsuyama, Iyo. Matsuyama also belonged to the shogunate party and was then in a state of despair.

In discussing the history of the period we must pay attention to the fact that those who embraced the new faith were those young people with the resolve to fight against society and to swim against the current of the times. They had no hope for the tiresome glories of this fleeting world. They had little hope for a good position in the material world.

Fukuzawa explained the feeling of people at the time:

> When the Restoration government established itself, not only all the former samurai in Japan but also the sons of farmers and the brothers of townsmen, if they had a little learning, wanted to become government officials. Even if they did not become government officials, they eagerly drew close to the government to try and make money. They were like flies around something that smells. People all over Japan thought that those who were not part of the government had no standing. There was no idea of being independent. There were any number of students returning from foreign studies who came to me boasting, "I am resolved to a lifelong commitment to independent study and have no thought of a government appointment." From the beginning I would listen tolerantly. I would not see the independent scholars for a long time, but later I would hear they had become clerks in some ministry, and those with good fortune had become provincial officials.
>
> The Restoration government was establishing a new household and it needed new people, so it was very generous in trying to win people over. Those who had the talent suitable for the new age were put to use at the discretion of the government. Those who until yesterday had viewed Satsuma and Choshu as enemies, and who had firmly resolved to support the shogunate party, frequently changed their plans and joined the ranks of the new government. No matter how generous the victors were, however, they could not abandon their conceit. No matter how warm a welcome the defeated received from the victors, they could not help but feel hurt by this conceit. Although the war became just an old story, in the hearts of the defeated there was a wound that still had not healed. The young people who praised the age or who progressed with the era's worldliness came largely from among the victors and their allies. Those who criticized the age and embraced the new creed that sought to fight against the age came largely from among the defeated. All spiritual revolutions come from the dark side of the age. The circumstance in which Christianity was first established in Japan was no exception to this rule.

At the time, there were some exceptions to this argument. Some people from Satsuma and Choshu who held high posts, like

Ōkubo Toshimichi and Saigō Takamori,[23] did become Christians. This was an example, however, of the elitist progressivism that occurred among the ruling elite. Most of those who threw themselves into evangelical work were the children of those who suffered adversity.

23. Ōkubo Toshimichi (1830–78) played a leading role in reforming his native domain of Satsuma before the Meiji Restoration and an equally significant part in the political events leading to the Restoration itself. After the Restoration he became one of the most powerful people in the new Meiji government, although his achievement was cut short by his early death at age forty-eight. Saigō Takamori (1827–77) was also a leading figure in the events that brought about the Meiji Restoration. After the Restoration in 1873, however, he resigned from the government following a bitter dispute concerning Japan's relations with Korea. He returned to his home area of Kagoshima, and in 1877 became the leader of the "Satsuma Rebellion" against the Meiji government. He committed suicide when the rebellion failed.

6

ON NAKAMURA MASANAO

At this time, the shogunate Confucianist Nakamura Masanao[24] was a trustworthy sympathizer of the young Japanese church, and he advocated many of the same ideas as the church. As a person he was selfless and good and his lifestyle was that of a scholar. He was not like Fukuzawa Yukichi, and he did not know the trick of blowing a trumpet and gathering many people together. He was not like Niijima Jō,[25] and he did not have the boldness of a volunteer prepared to die lying on the ground.

He was merely a scholar who read widely and assimilated what he read. He was not like Ogyū Sorai, who could single-handedly confront the universe and, fighting enemies on all sides, establish a new doctrine. He had the bravery of a person from Edo who coolly, disinterestedly, and without reserve spoke of his

24. Nakamura Masanao (1832–91) (also known by his pen name Nakamura Keiu) was a Confucian scholar who was sent to England before the Restoration in order to study Western culture. His translations of Samuel Smiles's (1812–1904) *Self Help* and John Stuart Mill's (1806–73) *On Liberty* were very influential in the early Meiji period. He was very sympathetic toward Christianity and was baptized in 1874, becoming the first prominent public figure to become a Christian.
25. Niijima Jō (1843–90) was the first ordained Protestant Japanese Christian and was the founder of Dōshisha College, which later became Dōshisha University. He secretly boarded a ship for the United States in 1864 and remained in the United States until 1874. In 1866 he was converted to Christianity and later studied at Amherst College and Andover Theological Seminary. While in America he assisted the Iwakura Mission, and after his return to Japan he was active as an educator and a missionary.

beliefs. He was not influenced by prejudice. He had the coolness of a person from Edo and was not moved by emotion. He had a wise head, cool judgment, and spoke of his beliefs without exaggeration, adornment, or hesitation.

With this kind of personality, he was sent by the shogunate to investigate English culture, and he saw that at the root of this culture was religion. He saw working vigorously within Christianity the principles of human nature and the way of heaven that his friend, Ōtsuki Bankei,[26] had found in the Chinese books he had studied for twenty years. He did not regard the teachings of Confucius as merely commonplace, but he thought that they were actually loftier and greater than those of Christianity, which had conquered Europe.

After the collapse of the shogunate that he had served, Nakamura had no choice but to return home. Even after his return he openly and without reservation showed sympathy for Christianity. His *Song of Love and Respect*, which was written at the time, shows the degree to which he inclined toward Christianity:

> We should devote ourselves to the ideals of love and respect.
> We should do this when times are good, but even in adversity
>   it will strengthen us.
> If you cannot succeed at a difficult task like correcting your
>   parents' stubbornness through love and respect, you can-
>   not understand the virtue of the sages.
> If you cannot succeed at a difficult task like making your lord
>   a virtuous ruler through love and respect, you cannot un-
>   derstand the deeds of the sages.
> The Western sage Socrates had a very stubborn wife.
> If he acted against her wishes, she lost her temper and would
>   not follow his orders about anything.
> If someone marries a young wife, she will always try to con-
>   trol him.
> Socrates said, "I am fortunate to marry this unreasonable
>   wife," as it will test and strengthen my love and respect.
> Science needs experiments to test its foundation, just as a
>   pine tree needs a strong wind to test its roots.

26. Ōtsuki Bankei (1801–78) was a Confucian scholar and educator who, in response to incursions into Japanese waters by foreign ships in the 1840s, advocated opening up the country to contact with the outside world.

Socrates is calm but his wife is emotional.

Socrates' calm is like a pond; his wife's emotions are like fire.

Later generations regarded Socrates as a sage simply because
of the depth of his love and respect.

The power of love and respect conquers everything.

Love and respect surpass the military power of steel warships
and armies of soldiers.

Love and respect are like links in a chain that have the capacity to tame wild animals.

Love and respect can pacify hatred between enemies.

The whole world should be one family and the universe
should have the same nature.

The things I wish for concern people in the present.

Subjects should be obedient, husband and wives harmoni-
ous, and friends warm.

All nations be careful about your relations and trust one another.

If this happens, a good star and a cloud of good fortune will
appear and they will shine on one another.

If you devote yourself to love and respect and serve your parents, virtue and morality will cover the whole world.

For thousands of years people have recited these words in
vain and even today we cannot see any result.

People learn about love and respect, but what they do comes
from greed and lust.

If there is one virtuous person, however, millions of others
will admire and follow him.

From a small unit like the family to a large unit like the state,
we should never be careless.

Listen carefully! God commands us to show love and respect.

For a long time Japanese attitudes were dominated by the
"expel the barbarian" principle. Foreigners were seen as very
depraved and their motives were deeply suspected. For this reason, a reaction against this way of thinking could not be avoided.
Yokoi Shōnan argued deductively from the theory of natural ability and intelligence that even foreigners were human beings. If
they were human beings with a conscience, why should they not
understand our sincerity? His arguments for foreign relations on
the basis of the unity of man was the first clear voice in this reaction. Nakamura Masanao's attempt to harmonize the teachings of
Christianity and Confucianism was a slight change of course, however, for those heading in this direction.

In 1871, Ono Azusa[27] produced a theory of the unity of the world:

> Now, as for a plan for the world, I support the establishment of one large federal government and the entrusting of the hopes of the world to wise men. A large parliament will be put in place to lead the world, and talented people from various places will establish laws, administer the world, and improve government. Those who do not improve the government will be punished. There will be popular education. From the beginning all the people of the world will join together, all will grow up together, and the rights of self-determination and freedom will be expanded. Will this not be a great blessing for the world?

Here you can see the birth of universalism in the heart of one young person.

That the reaction against the "expel the barbarian" slogan had reached this point clearly shows the trend of thought at the time. Nakamura Masanao was a representative of this intellectual trend. The basis of his argument was Christianized Confucianism, or, in other words, explaining Christianity from the perspective of Confucianism. From this point of view, he definitely stood at the head of the intellectual trend of the times. For young Christians, it was a good thing that he stood in a position of leadership.

At the same time that the church in Yokohama was built, Nakamura produced an essay called *A Paper Dedicated to the Emperor by a Certain Foreign Minister.* Using a pseudonym, he published this in a periodical called *Shinbun zasshi.* He argued that the court should use Western civilization and not only permit Christianity but encourage it, as it was the metaphysical element in Western civilization. It was for this reason that the hopes of Christians centered on Nakamura.

When one wave moves, all waves move. The activity of the small church had begun by fighting many obstacles. Some of the young people who belonged to the church had been forced to

---

27. Ono Azusa (1852–86) was a scholar who went to America and England in 1871 to study law, politics, and banking. He returned to Japan in 1874, and in 1876 he joined the government.

flee their homes because they were members of a heretical sect. Some had cut contacts with their teachers. Despite this they did not yield. Just as when water pressure breaks a stone covering a well, the water pushes out, so they were filled with the vitality of a new faith. They did not think of obstacles but followed their faith in a straight line. When you call out in a field, you will soon hear an echo. Christians soon became spoken of among lay people. Young people, who like novelty, soon began to visit the missionaries. The popularity of studying English at that time had the power to promote this vitality.

7

YASUI SOKKEN'S *AN EXPOSITION OF ERROR* I

The anxiety about the new religion was unending. The first person to strike a blow against Christianity was Yasui Sokken. He wrote a book called *An Exposition of Error* in which he argued that Christianity lacked credibility.

When I lived in Shizuoka and attended a Confucian school, I had not heard a lot about Christianity. At that time, however, I saw this book by Yasui on the desk of a friend, and after reading it, I was greatly impressed by his argument. I immediately took up my brush and wrote, "*An Exposition of Error* is a dynamic, five-volume book. I will treasure it greatly." This was twenty-two or twenty-three years ago. As a book it was rather old fashioned and could be bought only in second-hand book shops, so it was only the argument that I admired. I did not think of it then as a valuable souvenir that represented a certain period in Japanese intellectual history. Thinking back now, however, I believe this was the first criticism aimed at Christianity at the time the church was established in Japan. It was the most sagacious work in which the new faith was criticized on the basis of old Japanese thought. I think this book is very interesting in this sense, and for this reason I would like to discuss its contents.

Opening the book, first we touch on the introduction by Shimazu Hisamitsu:[28]

---

28. Shimazu Hisamitsu (1817–87), as the de facto ruler of Satsuma domain, played a leading role in national politics in the 1860s. After the Restoration, he served in the government for a short time but was largely ignored because of his extreme conservatism. In 1876 he resigned his government appointment and returned to Satsuma.

> Those who are devoted to Western teachings are also invari-
> ably devoted to Christianity and want to spread it to the inte-
> rior of Japan. This would be a disaster.

Shimazu was a representative of the conservative faction of the time, and he saw the vigor with which the Japanese people welcomed Christianity. He wrote that he could not look on indifferently to this situation, and he wished somebody would fight against it. Then he discovered that Yasui had already entered the field of battle. We can see from this that Christianity had reached the point where it had enough vigor, or was seen to have enough vigor, to worry the conservatives.

Having glanced at Shimazu Hisamitsu's introduction, I will advance to the appendix, in which Yasui writes on republicanism:

> Students of Western studies do not understand Confucian
> values, and they easily draw the conclusion that these values
> are useless. They fail to see that the teachings of Confucius
> can be used to distinguish between good and bad. Even when
> their seditious talk reaches the stage that they advocate re-
> publicanism, they do not realize that they have committed a
> serious crime. If they reach this stage, they do not cease their
> liking for heresy and become Christians. If they do not cease
> being Christians, they will become people without parents or
> lord. They are like people in an opium dream who enjoy their
> days but do not realize the harm. I lament this, but no amount
> of regret will mend matters. We must be careful.

In his view, republicanism and Christianity were almost the same thing. This new religion had come by ship and had thrown the Japanese intellectual world into confusion, but he did not ask if it was a religious faith or a political doctrine. According to Yasui, both Christianity and republicanism were similar forms of thought. This shows that he was unable to escape the conservative habit of hating all new things simply because they are new.

Entering the main text, however, I cannot help but greatly admire his attitude as a debater. He did not argue on the basis of emotion. First, he read Christian texts by himself; then, he read several books about Christianity; and, having digested these to a certain extent, he went on to make his attack.

8

YASUI SOKKEN'S *AN EXPOSITION OF ERROR* II

It must be said that Yasui's knowledge of Christianity was very narrow. He could not read Western writing, and therefore he could not read Western books on theology or philosophy. It cannot be said, however, that his knowledge of Christianity was inaccurate, like that of the later Inoue Tetsujirō. It is clear from his book that he read the Bible well and grasped the essential points of its teachings. For this one thing I admire him. His intellect was old, but his power was undiminished. First he studied Christianity, and after that he made his criticism.

His most incisive criticism was of the Old Testament. He wrote:

> I hear that God is spirit and has no form. God made all the things in heaven and earth in six days. God is that great! Is it not strange that he made something as insignificant as man in his own image?

This was a criticism of the idea in Genesis that man was made in the image of God. Again he wrote:

> God made Adam by getting dust together and giving this life. Eve was created by taking a rib from Adam and giving this flesh. This was the creation of mankind. For this, materials were necessary. God made all the things in heaven and earth. What did he use as materials for these things?

This is a criticism of the weakness of the account of the creation of matter found in Genesis. Again he wrote:

> Among living things, the snake is the craftiest. Could God not have made this? Why did he make the snake? The snake tempted Eve and got her to eat the fruit from the forbidden place.

This criticism relates to the cause of sin and shows that the explanation in the creation story is not at all accurate.

Again Yasui wrote:

> When Eve ate forbidden fruit she committed a crime. This was a crime she had to commit. The crime of Eve was the crime of all subsequent females. For this they must endure the hardship of childbirth. What a false accusation! All things that have blood have males and females. They are distributed evenly throughout all species. What crime have they committed? Why do females have to suffer from the pain of the womb? If Eve had never been made to eat the fruit from the forbidden place, she would not have had a baby. Then God could not have avoided getting more dust to make people. Was God afraid of going to the trouble?

This is a sharp criticism of the theory found in the creation story that the difficulty of childbearing is the result of sin.

Yasui then proceeded to the legend of Noah and the flood. With regard to this he argued that God lacked humanity. He also wrote that in China there was also a legend of a great flood in ancient times, so the story itself was true. In the Chinese case, however, there was no legend of the human race being wiped out, so he concluded that the legend of Noah was untrue. He laughed at the story of God mixing up human languages and at God interfering in the trivial family affairs of Abraham and Jacob.

He also criticized the cosmology of the creation myth and the idea of a "Great Abyss":

> The moisture from the sky fell down and moisture from the earth rose up. Was it at this time that rain began to fall? The sky was blue to look at. I do not know where the Great Abyss was.

Human hearts are the same everywhere. Eighteenth-century French philosophers engaged in biblical criticism on the basis of reason and scepticism. The same kind of criticism was first expressed in Japan by Yasui Sokken.

It must be said that Yasui did show up the weaknesses in the Christian teachings of the time. People have said, however, that this was merely because he did not understand what the creation myth really was. The account of the creation of the world is not a doctrinal or theological book. It is only one of the old legends preserved among the Jewish people. To criticize this logically is to mistake the nature of the document. The foreign missionaries at the time, however, did not teach this. Their teaching was that each word and each verse in the Bible was the word of God and there were no mistakes. They taught that even an account such as that of the creation of the world was no exception. It was about thirteen years after the publication of *An Exposition of Error* that I entered the church. The pastors, however, wanted to emphasize that the creation myth did not contradict recent geology, and I know they worked hard on this interpretation. They harbored no doubts and advocated the notion of "biblical inspiration." They would not consider any different opinion.

In other words, by accurately pointing out the falsehoods in the creation myth, Yasui struck at the main fault of those times. Of course, the church had a history of eighteen hundred years and had often encountered similar attacks. They could bring out arguments against these criticisms rather in the way somebody takes things out of a bag. The foreign missionaries could skillfully bring something out of the storehouse of apologetics to explain the doubts of the young believers and to stop discussion in the church. Young people outside the church, however, were moved by this book. They felt contempt for the new faith and stopped approaching the church.

9

YASUI SOKKEN'S *AN EXPOSITION OF ERROR* III

In the final chapters, Yasui's criticism becomes more incisive. He criticizes the account in which Jacob is said to have known of the seven-year famine:

> If Jacob knew of the seven-year famine, then God must also have known about it as well. God recommended a Sabbath day and also a Sabbath year every seven years, and he would not allow the people to work. There was a fear that they would not have enough to eat, so he said: "In the sixth year I will make enough food for two or three years." In this way the quality of the world's harvest is in God's mind. He is the master of heaven. In other words, the world's people are all his people. Why did he not turn famine into plenty to help them? Certainly they will use up all the things they have and will have to auction grain. Then Jacob will get a good reputation.

Yasui wrote that God was extremely cruel because, when Moses left Egypt, the Egyptians drowned in the Red Sea as a result of the stubbornness in the heart of the king. He argued that God's rewards and punishments were lacking in morality:

> Aaron made a gold calf, worshipped it, and was punished. A neighboring country followed another God and was destroyed. Korah opposed him, so he made the soil swallow him. Israel had two unmarried daughters. They plotted together, made their father drunk, and lay with him in turns. A widowed bride covered her face and, lying that she was a prostitute, slept with her father-in-law. A child resulted and this became pub-

lic knowledge. Was not the shame of this worse than the actions of animals? There was, however, no punishment. They were as licentious as they desired and were allowed to make fools of their parents.

In this way Yasui criticized the Bible. Then he made the following assessment:

> In the Bible, Noah was the first to serve God. Then there came Abraham and later Moses. Moses was a great villain. He used God's name to trouble the people. He raised an army. When he was not ready to attack, he said, "God does not permit it." When he saw that the time was right to attack, he said, "God will guide us." Suddenly, he thought of territorial expansion. In this book, they still had not come in contact with other people. The area recorded in this book is limited to a corner of Asia and Africa. This is the evidence.

Yasui had the insight to see that the age of the Old Testament was an age of national bias and that the religion of the Old Testament has a national bias. I must say that he clearly perceived what was written between the lines.

After he finished discussing the Old Testament, he moved to the New Testament. The first thing he noted was that Christ had contempt for the principle of loyalty and filial piety. He wrote:

> You should not love your mother and father more than me. You should not love your children more than me. Christ spoke to the people and he wished to say this to the mothers and brothers standing outside. A certain person questioned him. Christ said, "Who is our mother? Who is our brother?" He wished to show great fairness to that follower but he did not know that he himself had fallen into a great sin. A disciple's father had died and the disciple wished to bury him, but Jesus would not permit this, saying, "You follow me, leave the dead to bury the dead." I believe that serving one's father and burying one's father are the same thing.
>
> Jesus said, "If you follow me, your soul will have eternal life and will not die." With regard to people, he thought of as unimportant those who are called rulers. He did not teach a doctrine that explained the reason for following one's ruler. Not only did he not teach the reason we must follow our ruler, but if there was a ruler who did not believe in him, he called

him an enemy. He wished to defeat those rulers and have them submit to him. He regarded tax collectors as robbers. If we trace back the origin of this idea it is because he regarded rulers as his enemy. He called himself the son of the master of heaven. He thought society should revere him. Therefore, his disciple Peter replied to someone who criticized him, and who worshipped the (worldly) ruler, by saying, "We do not know the kings and gods of the underworld and we worship only the Lord of Heaven. We believe in paying tax to the king with money and we respect him as the king but we do not bend our knee to him. Though we pay tax and have a king, we give thanks to the Lord."

At about this time, there was a person who murdered his lord. He said he was a false lord, and he respected his true lord. If we punish the false lord for Christ, this is real love for the true Lord and it is for the glory of God. The more severe the punishment, the greater the glory. In this way he led the people and the people feared this. Was there profit for him in this? For someone who follows these ideas, it is not contrary to the teachings of Christ even to act against their ruler. Even if you injure the flesh for as long as one hundred years, you do not lose the eternal glory of heaven. If it reaches the point where someone is under the influence of this kind of spell, threats of punishment are insufficient. Status and money are insufficient to persuade them. This is a difficult situation for rulers.

Various intelligent Roman emperors made the same criticism of Christianity as Yasui, and they persecuted Christians. Ten years after Yasui, Professor Inoue Tetsujirō argued in the same way that Christianity was incompatible with the national polity and harmful to education. Not only did this kind of criticism exist among scholars but, in reality, Christians had sometimes fought against rulers in the name of God. It is clear from the history of the Puritans that, at times, Christianity had been used as a pretext for murdering kings. The Shimabara Uprising[29] showed that at times the Christian church had encouraged the bravery of rebels. Criti-

---

29. The Shimabara Uprising was a peasant rebellion that broke out in 1673. Although the causes were largely economic, the Shimabara-Amakusa area had been a stronghold of Christianity before its suppression by the Tokugawa, and the rebellion was partly inspired by Christianity. It was ruthlessly suppressed by the Tokugawa and was the last major military threat to their rule before the conflict leading to the Meiji Restoration.

cizing Christianity on this basis, however, must be considered unfair.

Try thinking! Mencius was a proponent of the theory of the innate goodness of man, and he never tired of speaking of goodness and humanity. By arguing for the death sentence for King Chu, did he not give a pretext for later generations of usurpers? According to Chinese scholars, the *Shu ching* is a record of the great scriptures and great laws of the sages. Did not later generations, however, use the records of abdication and banishment as a pretext for killing their rulers? Buddhism also has the teachings of meekness and forgiveness. The followers of the Ikkō sect, however, sometimes fought against their rulers, contrary to the teachings of Buddhism.[30] Did not Rai San'yō argue that the Hōjō[31] destroyed any feeling of shame concerning disloyalty or unfilial conduct on the basis of the Zen religion? Lao Tsu taught that if sages did not die, then criminals would not die either. He also taught that if you break the measuring rods and burn the measuring scales, then people will stop fighting. Can anyone doubt that this is anarchism? I have not yet heard, however, of any clever politician using the power of the state to suppress this anarchism.

There is a great difference between principles and practice. As Lord Macaulay[32] has written, all teachings and all philosophy, if they are taken to their theoretical extreme, would destroy the existing social order. In reality, however, this kind of thought is like seeing a comet and worrying about the danger of a forest fire. If filial relations themselves are strengthened, there is no need to fear that such relations will be destroyed from within, even if there were a hundred religions like Christianity. If the

---

30. The Ikkō Ikki were large-scale uprisings of the 15th and 16th centuries by adherents of the Jōdō Shin sect of Buddhism. In one rebellion the military governor of Kaga Province was killed, and members of the sect took over control of the province, which they retained for nearly a century.

31. Rai San'yō (1781–1832) was a historian and poet principally known for his book *Nihon gaishi* (An Unofficial History of Japan), which was the most popular history of Japan in the nineteenth century. Rai San'yō was critical of military families such as the Hōjō (and by implication the Tokugawa), who, he believed, had usurped imperial authority.

32. Thomas Babington Macaulay (1800–59) was an English historian and politician influential among liberal Japanese intellectuals in the early and mid-Meiji period.

ethics concerning filial relations are established by heaven, Christianity teaches respect for heaven. Respecting heaven involves valuing the morals established by heaven. I cannot respect Yasui's theory that Christianity is contrary to the principles concerning filial relations. The ethics involved in these relationships are not based on religion but on the simple interrelationships that exist among people, or at least we may suppose that they are. To emphasize that the ethical relationship between the ruler and ruled and between parents and children is established by heaven is to emphasize that it is a truth, not an expediency.

Yasui criticized Christianity for disloyalty and lack of filial piety, but I must say that this was an unreasonable criticism. This was not, however, his voice alone. I have read many criticisms of Christianity by Confucian scholars at the time that Christianity was introduced to China during the Ming period. The focus of criticism is on this point. I have also read a book by the Mito scholar, Aizawa Seishisai,[33] written at the end of the Edo period, in which he criticized Christianity. I know that his ideas were the same. Yasui's argument was elegant and incisive, and for this reason it can be regarded as being representative, even though it is wrong. The fact that Yasui saw Christianity as a danger in this way shows that he had some reason other than simply its teachings. His book indicates that he regarded Christianity as persistent, destructive, confusing, and sowing the seeds of destruction.

Yasui wrote:

> Jehovah called himself a jealous God and would not permit his followers to worship another God. Christ emphasized this more and more, saying he would destroy other gods. For this reason, he said, "I do not come to bring peace but to cause strife." Should this religion be adopted, the shrines of Emperor Jinmu and of the various emperors and nobles and those dedicated to patriots and illustrious men will have to be destroyed. The whole nation down to the ordinary samurai and lower classes will have to give up offering services to the souls

---

33. Aizawa Seishisai (1782–1863) served Tokugawa Nariaki, the lord of the Mito domain, and in this capacity was influential in shaping the domain's policy in the late Tokugawa period. His book *Shinron* inspired many proimperial activists at the time.

of their parents and ancestors. Can our custom of filial piety
endure such a thing? I hear that in the West, believers are
divided between old and new. In America, Christianity is divided into twenty-five groups. These groups all fight with
one another without apology. If somebody fights for some
other reason and later asks for peace, then this is agreed to. If
they mobilize troops for religious reasons, they will not accept surrender. This kind of war ends in massacre. With this
so-called teaching they rule the people and try to bring peace
to the world. Now these religious groups fight each other, kill
each other, and try to destroy other types of belief. Why do
they fight for their beliefs? They are the same Christian religion but they fight over some tiny differences. They kill each
other without apology. This slaughter is their so-called teaching. They exhaust themselves in attacking others and wish to
destroy their opponents. We, however, have Shintoists. Although their power is weak, they believe in deities and their
teachings are based on this. If the Christians and Shintoists
all come together, there will be fighting among the people
without end.

This is to see nineteenth-century Christianity as the era of the
Crusades, the era of the Reformation, or the era of Xavier Loyola.
This is to see the tolerant and free Christianity of the nineteenth
century as the Christianity of an age in which, in the name of
God, those who preached heresy were burned and people of other
sects were killed. This is the point of view from which Yasui saw
Christianity and argued about its principles. Why did he feel this
danger? In the Tenpō period, the noted Confucian Koga Dōan[34]
had written *A Speculation on Coastal Defense,* and in it he had explained that the era of religious wars was a thing of the past in the
West. I respect Dōan's views and regret that, after Dōan, Yasui
did not have enough insight to understand the age. The weakness of Yasui's book is that he did not understand the times and
he did not understand the Christianity of the period. His weakness was not that he did not have the ability to criticize the Bible.

He argued with regard to the crucifixion that Christ himself did not want to go to the place of execution:

---

34. Koga Dōan (1788–1847) was a Confucian scholar of the late Tokugawa period who
taught at the shogunate's official academy, the Shōheikō.

> If Christ wished to redeem sins through his death, on the
> evening before his death he should have been quiet and not
> worried. He was not able to sleep on the final night, however.
> He awoke his disciples and told them this. Judas had sold his
> life for thirty pieces of silver, but Jesus did not know about
> this himself. He did not know that Judas had sold him but
> chose him as one of the twelve disciples. This was extreme
> ignorance! Also, did he not know that his blood would flow to
> redeem the sins of the people?

Yasui suggests that this is evidence that there is no teaching of redemption, because Christ's death could not be stopped. He also complained that there were contradictions with regard to eternal life:

> Christ died and was resurrected, and he met his disciples and
> preached to them. Christ spoke of eternal life without death,
> and especially he spoke of the spirit. If the flesh decayed, it
> could not be resurrected. With this idea he encouraged his
> followers. Only he himself, however, resurrected his body. Is
> not this to praise the body and despise the spirit? Christ rose
> into heaven. Heaven was only the sky. Even though he resur-
> rected his body, where did he put his feet? It is clear that he
> did not take his body. When Christ died, he said in a loud
> voice, "Father, I entrust my spirit unto you. I go to my fa-
> ther." Why did he not say I entrust my body to you? If Christ
> had come in contact with many people after he had resur-
> rected his body as a manifestation of God, more people would
> have believed his teachings. He spoke only, however, to his
> disciples and to some old women. Ordinary people could not
> help but be doubtful. Why did Christ not try to get across to
> more people?

Yasui wrote in this way, and even today people with common sense who read the Bible cannot help but feel the same way. I must say that he clearly attacked the difficult points of the so-called ortho-dox teachings.

10

Yasui Sokken's View of the Universe

Before ending my critique of *An Exposition of Error*, I must discuss Yasui's view of the universe. The shaping of Confucianism as a systematic philosophy began with *The Doctrine of the Mean*. The author of *The Doctrine of the Mean* unified the laws of the universe with human nature. The laws of the universe are expressed concretely in human nature, so that when human nature is trained, there is no contradiction with the universe. Speaking from the perspective of mankind, this is to achieve the purpose of life; speaking from the perspective of the universe, it is to achieve the purpose of the universe. In other words, combining human nature with the Way, is the Way of Heaven. Starting from this kind of philosophical point of view, there is a natural division into two kinds of philosophical systems. If you explain the development of the universe beginning with human nature, then the universe is spirit. If you seek the source of human nature beginning with the universe, then human nature is material. Putting this in other words, if you put emphasis on the Way of Heaven as the philosophy of *The Doctrine of the Mean*, then it is materialistic. If you emphasize human nature, then it is spiritualistic. You cannot escape these two trends within Confucianism. Within the Confucian tradition, Wang Yang-ming tended toward spiritualism, and Yasui, toward materialism. Why do I say this?

Look at the way Yasui explains the origin of things:

The sun is the center for the earth and the five stars. They turn in empty space by day and night. Each has its place. The earth turns in one day. About 366 turns is the circumference of the sun. This is one year. There are four seasons, twelve months, twenty-four fifteen-day periods, and seventy-two five-day periods. All derive their name from the distance of the sun. All things have size, all things grow old, all things end. There is no matter in the places where spirit does not reach. Everything is fixed for eternity and does not change its place. The sun is the master of the earth and has always been so. Things that exist, however, wax and wane. Thus, it is possible to say that the sun created the earth. This is also the same for the five stars. Insects appeared from ash and fish appeared from stagnant water. Human life began and acquired spirit. The spirit of Yang became the male and the spirit of Yin became the female. Males and females were separated. They were evenly distributed and the species grew abundantly. This was not just the case for human beings. The earth is the center for the moon. It revolves every twenty-nine days. In this way heaven protects the earth. For this reason, we feel the influence of the Yin principle. Flesh follows the waxing and the waning of the moon. Ebb and flow follow the advance and retreat of the moon. This is clear. Women have the principle of Yin. For this reason, they have menstruation once a month but only four months a year and three days a month. In this way the moon strongly influences men and women. We cannot doubt this. The spirit is created with flesh. It grows with age, just as the body becomes larger with years. We do not receive our bodies from our parents and later receive our spirit from God.

Yasui had still not heard of the Western theory of materialism. He had not read Bain. He had not read Tyndall and Huxley.[35] In his philosophy there was a vapor that acted as a bridge and transformed matter and spirit. It united them. This is pure materialism. Even in regard to his theory of gender, he clearly employed a materialistic interpretation.

He wrote:

The conscience of the spirit is the master of the body. For this reason, taste occurs in the mouth, color appears to the

---

35. Alexander Bain (1818–1903), John Tyndall (1820–93), and Thomas Huxley (1825–95) were all prominent nineteenth-century British scientists.

eyes, a voice comes to the ear, smell comes to the nose, relaxation comes to the body. First we experience something physical and then the spirit begins. Christ had a body and was strong willed, but still he could not make his ear speak or his eyes listen. If the body declines, there is no contact with material things; the five desires and the seven emotions do not work. Christians explain this in the following way: "If there is joy or pain in a dream, then the spirit also has joy or pain." I do not understand this. When you have a dream, this develops from the body. I still have not heard of a dream in which the neck walks and the foot holds things. Where there is no body there are no dreams. In other words, the emotions control the body; pain and pleasure come from the emotions. If the spirit is separated from the flesh, then it is clear there is no pain or pleasure.

In other words, after the body dies there is no spirit. Even if there is, according to this explanation, it experiences no pain or pleasure. Yasui's heart was extremely materialistic and this-worldly.

He was a hermit and lived in seclusion. He was someone who represented the old era and was not someone who understood the new era. The materialism and this-worldliness of his argument reflected one aspect of his age. I wonder if the winds of this transient world never blew into the quiet retreat of this old teacher or tempted his heart!

11

On Niijima Jō

If you evaluate Yasui's book against the intellectual standards of the day, it was an extraordinary masterpiece. His criticism of the Bible was enough to make Christians inquire deeply into their own faith. The young people of the time who chased after new ideas as if they were starving, however, did not have the appropriate attitude to listen carefully to the arguments of an old Confucian scholar. First of all, they had a deep belief in and reverence for Western civilization. They believed that Christianity was the pillar that supported that civilization. They believed too much in Western civilization to be moved by one book. They were too busy to meditate on the words of an old Confucian. The foreign missionaries, seeing that their hearts inclined toward Christianity, gave them religious training unceasingly in order to cultivate and develop their faith. A work produced through the earnest efforts of a Confucian teacher was useless in trying to block the flow of Christianity.

At the time that the young church was developing in Japan and new believers were joining in various places, Niijima Jō was graduating from Amherst College in America and becoming a missionary of the Congregationalist Church. He thought of Christianity continuously, and he returned to Japan to begin missionary work.

Niijima Jō was a samurai from Kosuke domain. He was one of those Japanese who was greatly aroused by the events in the world. He expressed his desire in the following way: "I wanted to bravely volunteer, go abroad, and undertake the great task of seeing other countries." At the time of the Restoration, the promising young heart of this person was stirred up, and through the recommendation of the progressive politician Itakura Katsukiyo (the lord of Matsuyama domain in Bichu),[36] he got tacit consent to leave his domain and stowed away on a boat. He went over to America. He explained the events of the time himself:

> One day, when I was walking along in Edo, I happened to meet a friend on his way to Tamashima. He told me that his lord's ship would be weighing anchor and leaving in three days for Hakodate. He urged me to travel with him. It was only the invitation of an acquaintance, but it was something I was interested in. After I left my friend, a new desire struck like lightening and illuminated my heart. I secretly resolved to take this lucky opportunity of being able to go over to Hakodate to put into effect my long-cherished desire. Even if I consulted my former lord, I could not see how he would permit me to travel. For this reason, first of all, I told Lord Matsuyama. I wanted to complete this plan without letting my parents or former lord know. I immediately visited one of the trusted retainers of Lord Matsuyama. I described my circumstances and petitioned him for help. He was a friend so he greatly praised my plan. He immediately went to the mansion with my request and explained the situation. Lord Matsuyama was also greatly pleased with my plan. He sent a messenger to the lord of my domain to secure my freedom. My lord, who met this kind messenger, had no reason to refuse, so I received my freedom. This was the beginning of my plan. There was no obstacle to hinder me from going to Hakodate. My father heard the news, and he did not want me to go because of the feeling that exists between parent and child. After my former lord gave permission, however, there was no reason to stop me. Two days after this was settled, my traveling clothes were ready as a result of the great efforts of my grandmother and my sister. My grandfather invited my friends and acquaintances to a banquet to ensure the success of my trip. When all the principal guests were settled, my grandfather first offered a toast, saying it would be difficult

36. Itakura Katsukiyo (1823–89) was a senior counselor in the shogunate active in the areas of foreign affairs and finance. He was a close adviser to the last shogun, Tokugawa Yoshinobu.

to see each other again. The whole group was sad and nobody raised their heads. Only grandfather and myself looked
at each other intently. Grandfather was choked with tears in
his heart, but he wore a smile on his face. I also could not
show any sadness. At the end of the banquet, grandfather said
to me, "Your future is like climbing a flower-covered mountain peak. You cannot describe the pleasure. You must go
bravely toward your goal without entertaining any fear." I had
never dreamt of hearing this piece of advice from my grandfather. I was touched by this brave farewell speech, and it
took a lot of bravery to say good-bye to my friends and ac-
quaintances, my parents, sister, and the grandfather I respected with a sense of gratitude. I resolved not to return
home until I had accomplished my long-held dream of seeing
the world. Later, I became a lone traveler very far from the
home where I had been accustomed to live for so many years.

It was the time when Narushima Ryūhoku[37] wrote:

> For half my life I have tried to achieve a difficult task.
> My anger is like the shouts of soldiers in the night.
> The wind and waves of the Black Sea.
> The moon over the Red Sea.

It was at this time that Keiō College first acquired a copy of the
large *Webster's Dictionary* and treasured it as a sacred text. Niijima
Jō experienced the spirit of the times the same way that migrat-
ing birds experience their surroundings. When he first set foot on
American soil, he was like a successful Yoshida Shōin.[38] When he
left Japan he wrote:

37. Narushima Ryūhoku (1837–84) was a journalist, essayist, and critic. Before the Meiji
    Restoration he wrote a collection of anecdotes about Edo's red-light district that he
    later used as the first part of his major work *Ryūkyō shinshi* (1859–60). After the
    Restoration he worked for an antigovernment newspaper satirizing contemporary
    society and government, especially the bureaucracy.
38. Yoshida Shōin (1830–59) was a scholar, writer, expert in military arts, and ideologue
    of the "revere the emperor and expel the barbarian" movement of the late Edo
    period. In 1854 he attempted to stow away on Commander Perry's flagship with the
    intention of familiarizing himself with conditions in the West. In addition to writing
    extensively, Yoshida Shōin also opened a private school, and among his students
    were several people who were later to become the leaders of the Meiji Restoration,
    including Itō Hirobumi and Yamagata Aritomo. He was executed in 1859 as a part of
    the Ansei Purge, after an unsuccessful attempt to assassinate a senior shogunal fig-
    ure. Although unsuccessful in his goals, Shōin became a great source of inspiration
    for others.

When a samurai begins a task,
He will not give up until it is finished,
Even if I only have old clothes and my sword,
I will boldly think of world affairs.
I have a great ambition,
I will not rest until I have seen the five continents.

Was this the way of speaking of a religious pilgrim? No, he set out to see the world with the brave spirit of the so-called political activist of the pre-Restoration period.

Even though he boldly set out on this ambitious undertaking, surely he must have been astounded when he heard about the revolution in his home country. He had not been in America long when he heard the news that the shogunate army had been defeated by the soldiers of Satsuma and Choshu. Annaka domain sat on the fence, did nothing, and lost out to others. He heard of the miserable fate of his protector, Lord Matsuyama. He felt his desire for fame suddenly freeze like ice. Seeing that he was worried, the Hardy family, which had looked after and protected him, made him feel the great warmth of Christianity. He was greatly influenced by the free, democratic, and Christian America of the time. He resolved to return to his home country and seek a new destiny as a disciple of freedom and Christianity.

Among the missionaries of the Japanese church, he was particularly brilliant. He added Christian training to his qualities as a warm person. Before he received Christian training, he had the purity of a Japanese samurai. When he first set out for America, during the voyage, he felt his dignity as a samurai affronted, and he felt ashamed. In anger, he took out his sword and wished to die in order to save his honor. During the trip, he had to do manual work, and he accidentally threw the captain's spoon into the sea. With no attempt to conceal this, he went to the captain's room and apologized for his mistake. Taking out some money he had brought along with him, he asked the captain to accept it as recompense. Also, while they were at sea, he wished to buy a copy of the Bible that had been translated into Chinese. He took his short sword to the captain and asked to buy it for eight American dollars. The captain readily gave his consent, and he gladly bought it. Even when he unwillingly received the protection of the Hardy family, he wanted to maintain his dignity as a samurai; he did not become obliged to anyone unless it was absolutely necessary. His personality was already that of a brave and noble gentleman. He valued honor, he respected independence, and his courage could not be broken. While he was in Japan, he had a moral attitude toward both his family and friends. He took this morality with him to America. He became an enthusiastic Christian and at the same time became an enthusiastic believer in freedom and democracy. For this reason, he was different from other missionaries. Also, after he returned to Japan and began his work, young people with an interest in Christianity admired and respected him for this reason.

This was not strange. When he was introduced to the first Japanese government emissaries—Iwakura, Ōkubo, and Kido—he did not bow to them according to the traditional Japanese custom. Instead, he greeted them in an egalitarian American way. This was a decision that came naturally from someone with his kind of personality. At this time he made it known that he did not wish the twelve students who were studying abroad at the expense of the Japanese government to do the same thing. This was because he believed himself to be an independent person who had been brought up in a free society. The strength of his feeling can be seen clearly in a letter he sent to Mr. Flint at the time:

> Recently when Minister Mori met Mr. Hardy, he requested a list of the expenses paid out so far for my education. He said to Mrs. Hardy that it was regrettable that the expenses paid out so far had not been reimbursed. I do not want Mr. Hardy to hand over such a list. If the minister pays all the expenses, I will not be able to avoid the restraints of the Japanese government. I am a free person of Japan. I merely want to offer myself for Our Lord's purpose. I request that you meet Mr. Hardy as soon as possible and explain the situation. I will pray to God to give me prudence and wisdom to make this decision.

We can understand how the free and independent spirit of America affected him. With these qualities and these ambitions, he returned home after a long absence.

12

Contrasting Social Phenomena

I know there existed here a great social contrast. Look! At this time a high flier in the Japanese political world, the young politician Itō Hirobumi, went to Paris. This was the center of Western civilization, and he soon wanted to enter into fashionable games:

> The Iwakura Mission arrived in Paris. They went to a certain umbrella shop to buy an umbrella. The shop attendant was a beautiful girl of eighteen or nineteen. She met the customers and asked, "Are you Japanese?" Somebody replied, "Yes, we are." Then she said, "Then perhaps you know Monsieur Itō?" "Itō is traveling with us. How is it that you know Itō?" The beautiful girl laughed but did not answer. The person was confounded and said, "How is it that Hirobumi is so quick?" (From *Meiji goketsudan*)

In a small book Narushima Ryūhoku wrote of the gay quarters in Tokyo. He satirized the politicians of the great domains who, with the energy of victors, had thrown the public morals of old Edo into confusion by going to the gay quarters and causing trouble. They had become drunk on the glory of a spring day. But look! Next to them is somebody like Niijima Jō, who expects to spend his whole life as a missionary with no place to live peacefully, kneeling in a secret room praying to God. The men of Satsuma and Choshu had a great mission in Japanese history. Now they have accomplished that mission. There is much sadness in a situation where pleasure is taken to an extreme. The children of

the defeated were thrown into the dark side of the age and, together with those young people who felt the same way, looked
outside of enterprises and utility and longed for the light of a spiritual revolution. The contrast was like that between a spring field
in which the peach blossoms are already dying and a winter field
full of expectancy for the coming of spring. I cannot overlook this
social contrast.

13

THE PLEDGE OF MOUNT HANAOKA

To explain why this contrast came into being, you must return to the law of reaction that exists in the human heart. The incident in which this law of reaction was most clearly demonstrated was the pledge of Mount Hanaoka in Kumamoto.[39] This event happened about one year after Niijima Jō returned to Japan. It was a strange incident that seemed to foretell good fortune for the small Japanese church that had been progressing one step at a time up until then. What evidence do I have to say that in explaining the Mount Hanaoka pledge we must return to the law of reaction that exists in the human heart?

I ask the reader not to regard me as one who places too much emphasis on the links in human history. In explaining human affairs, I do not like to rely on mechanical causes simply saying "cause-effect" or "action-reaction." I believe that within history there is mystery. I believe that in human affairs there is the will of God. In the case of an incident that can be explained by a mechanical cause, however, there is no need to add the notion of mystery. A very religious person would say that an incident like the pledge of Mount Hanaoka was due to the providence of heaven

---

39. In 1876 a group of thirty-five young men climbed Mount Hanaoka on the outskirts of Kumamoto and signed a document pledging themselves to work for Christianity. Among the "Kumamoto Band" were several who became prominent Christian leaders, including Ebina Danjō (1856–1937), Kanamori Tsūrin (1857–1945), Kozaki Hiromochi (1856–1938), and Yokoi Tokio (1857–1927).

or came from the grace of the Holy Spirit. I will not search for the
ultimate cause of the event at present, but, speaking as a historian, I will say that the direct cause was the law of reaction in the
human heart.

In Kyushu at that time, educated young people liked to
discuss politics. If they did not become government officials, then
they joined in the opposition's plans to take over the government.
This kind of political atmosphere was particularly strong in Kumamoto. Why do you often see two or three branches of peach blos-
som in front of bamboo? It is the reaction of the human heart that
becomes tired of seeing only the green of bamboo. The desire of
a group of young people in Kumamoto to throw themselves into
the religious world was merely the result of a reaction of the same
kind.

With the exception of the Ogasawara, who fought for the
Tokugawa and had the unfortunate fate of having their domain
almost destroyed, most of the domains in Kyushu, to a greater or
lesser degree, were in the position of victors over the shogunate.
The attitude of Saga was vague at the beginning, but together
with the three domains of Satsuma, Choshu, and Tosa, it became
one of the four pillars of the Restoration government. Among the
domains in Kyushu, Kumamoto alone was pushed into a relatively
disadvantageous position. The Kumamoto domain followed
Kagoshima in size. Literary activity was very strong there, and
Kumamoto was without comparison in western Japan. There were
many talented people there, so it was respected by the other domains. It was the strongest region for literature during the Tokugawa period. Behind the appearance of a country samurai dressed
in a rustic coat, there was an aesthetic sentiment: the sight of a
flower could express the idea of yearning poetically, or the sight
of the moon could depict love. The people of Edo could not de-
spise Kyushu. There was a lingering memory of and respect for
Yusai, Sansai, and Gindai.[40] Their home towns were Mizutari,

40. Hosokawa Yusai (also known as Fujitaka, 1534–1610) was a warlord who supported
     Oda Nobunaga. After Oda's death he retired from political and military affairs and
     concerned himself with cultural pursuits. He was known as an outstanding author-
     ity on waka poetry. Hosokawa Sansai (also known as Tadaoki, 1563–1646) was Yusai's

Hakusen; Akiyama, Gyokuzan; Yabu, Kozan; Karashima, Ensei; Kinoshita, Shikin, and these were the best places in Kyushu for literature. As Shibano Ritsuzan,[41] one of the "three scholars of the Kansei period," wrote, places that excel in literature and debate are weak in self-restraint and unity.

Kumamoto did not follow a wise policy in the Restoration, and it did not receive appropriate treatment as one of the great domains of Kyushu. This hurt the feelings of the people in Kumamoto, and for this reason many of them looked askance at the new age and were dissatisfied with it.

Looking at the national situation, there was the dispute over the invasion of Korea, the withdrawal of Saigō, and the petition for a parliament. Then there came the disturbance in Saga, the meeting in Osaka, and the imperial edict to establish constitutional government. The situation gradually began to settle down. Then, there was the end of the union between Shimazu Hisamitsu of the conservative party and Itagaki Taisuke of the progressive party.[42] The government was surrounded and attacked by both the conservative and the progressive parties. There were signs that society would fall into chaos. At this time, the people in Kumamoto were hearing news of the Saigō group in Satsuma in the south. In the north of Kyushu, discontented groups were also conspiring. The things that these people were trying to do were natural. One extreme, however, produces another extreme. Sud-

---

son. He was also a supporter of Oda Nobunaga but later switched allegiance, first to Toyotomi Hideyoshi, and then to Tokugawa Ieyasu. After the Battle of Sekigahara he was awarded a domain in what is now Fukuoka and Oita Prefectures in Kyushu. Tadaoki was also a poet, painter, and expert on etiquette and ceremony. Hosokawa Gindai (also known as Tadatoshi, 1586–1641), Tadaoki's son, was transferred to a fief in Kumamoto in 1632, and this was the beginning of the Hosokawa family's links with the region.

41. Shibano Ritsuzan (1736–1807) was a Confucian scholar of the Edo period. He is regarded as being responsible for the 1790 edict making knowledge of Zhu Xi Confucianism as taught by the Hayashi family a prerequisite for entering the shogunate administration. Along with Bitō Nishū (1745–1813) and Okada Kansen (1740–1816), he is referred to as one of the "three scholars of the Kansei period."

42. Itagaki Taisuke (1837–1919) was the leader of the Freedom and Popular Rights movement in the 1870s and 1880s and was the founder of Japan's first major political party, the Jiyūtō (Liberal Party).

denly there appeared in an area that had this kind of heavy political atmosphere a group professing a new faith and for this purpose wishing to fight a spiritual war.

Just as in other large domains where foreigners had been hired before this, in Kumamoto an American called Captain Janes[43] had been employed at the recommendation of the missionary Verbeck.[44] He taught the students at the domain school and, even after the domain was abolished, continued teaching the children at the school as before. Captain Janes, like many other foreigners employed at various places at the time, taught Christianity when he had time free from teaching English. Gradually the number of students who were moved by what he said increased. These young people gathered together on Mount Hanaoka in a suburb of Kumamoto in the spring of 1876 and pledged to bring about a spiritual revolution.

One member of this group was Kozaki Hiromichi, and he later explained the situation at the time:

> The way I first became a Christian is a very old story. It is not well known, but at the time of the Restoration, even in my domain of Kumamoto, capable people had to be trained, and there was a school of Western studies. At the domain's expense, a school was built and an American military officer was employed. At first, he correctly taught English. The students in the school were those chosen from among the young people in the domain who had the greatest talent and the best prospects. They studied at the domain's expense, so in the first term there were only a few students. In the second and third terms there were fifty or sixty students, and I was fortunate enough to be selected as one of them. The English teacher was a very enthusiastic believer, and while I was studying at the school, there gradually appeared among the students

43. Leroy Lansing Janes (1838–1909) was a graduate of the United States Military Academy who had participated in the Civil War. He came to Japan in 1871 and was responsible for the program of studies at Kumamoto domain's school of Western studies until the school was forced to close in 1876.
44. Guido Verbeck (1830–98) was a Dutch-born American missionary who was sent to Nagasaki by the Dutch Reform Church in 1859. In addition to his proselytizing activity, he also taught English, social sciences, and Western technology. Among his students were people such as Itō Hirobumi and Ōkubo Toshimichi, who went on to become leading figures in the Meiji government.

people who read the Bible. As for me, my family was Confucian, so I never inclined that way. My friends often recommended that I read the Bible. At last, I tried reading it. I had some doubts, and anguish, too, but finally I discovered certainty, and then came peace of mind. From then until now, I have never changed my belief in one God. I have never moved from my belief that this is the right faith, the true teaching, and the true way. All the believers gathered together and made a pledge to each other. We thought that entering politics or the army might be suitable work, but still we felt that it was too low class, and also there were many people who already did such work. We wanted work that the majority of people could not do. We decided to put our efforts into the spiritual world to awaken confused minds, to correct them, and to lead them to the true road. We would not give up no matter what hardships or calamities we experienced.

This was our departure into the world of religion. This event gradually became publicly known. In the domain, or more exactly, among the relatives of the students, there was great surprise. It would not do, people said, to study and become Christian clergymen. There was an uproar and it was said that it was an insult to the throne. Following this the school was closed and we were placed in the custody of our relatives. As for me, I did not have a father, so there was not so much of a row. Of course, my mother was greatly worried, but she said I had done nothing bad and that from now on I planned to do something good, so she would not worry. My mother understood very well and I had no especially difficult relatives, so I was able to proceed as I intended. Among my comrades, however, there was a great commotion. Yokoi Tokio, for example, came from a Confucian family, and his mother said that such a thing was an insult to his ancestors and an insult to the domain lord. Above all, there would be nothing she could say to her dead husband. His mother threatened to kill herself. Then he was turned over to his uncle, who was a teacher in a Chinese school. He also tried to get him to change his mind, but Yokoi refused to move. He was shut out of the house and there was a great uproar.

Another of our comrades was a person called Yoshida. His father was strong, and thus he drew out his sword and threatened to kill Yoshida. When his father did this, Yoshida stuck out his neck saying, "It cannot be avoided because of my belief." His father, who had only planned to frighten him into changing his ways and had no plans to kill him, shouted "You fool," and kicked him off the verandah and went inside. Tokutomi Sohō and so on were still young, so they had no choice but to change following their father's advice. A fire was lit in the garden and all the Bibles were burnt. For Kanamori Tsūrin and Ebina Danjō, there was also a great commotion of the same kind. (From *Shunbukyo*)

The young people of Kyushu knew nothing except becoming government officials or else joining the Popular Rights movement. Among those people, only the Kumamoto Band took upon itself the responsibility for bringing about a spiritual revolution. In the Kanto region, there were also the children of the defeated or those who had been put in the same position as the defeated. Taking responsibility for a spiritual revolution was a phenomenon that concerned both eastern and western Japan. From this time, Christianity gradually took root in the heart of the Japanese people. Fighting with various kinds of obstacles, the small church expanded its base day by day.

14

The First Reaction against
Westernization—Fukuzawa Yukichi

At this time a very unfavorable intellectual current began to flow
against the young church. This was an extreme reaction against
Westernization. In the early Meiji period, the majority of progressive people had advocated the pure imitation of the West. This
phenomenon, however, did not last long. After people studied the
West deeply, they understood that Western civilization had deep
roots and a long history. Japan could not become like the West in
a short period of time. In other words, some of these people gradually approached a kind of national consciousness. I cannot judge
exactly when this reaction began to grow in their hearts. You could
see signs of it in many different areas. The Ministry of Education's
Dr. Murray,[45] who had been brought over from America by Tanaka
Fujimaro,[46] argued that preservation of the national language was
preservation of nationality. This countered the extreme argument
of Mori Arinori. Katō Hiroyuki's argument that the formation of a
national parliament was premature can also be seen as another
argument of this kind. Kido Takayoshi's theory of gradual politi-

---

45. David Murray (1830–1905) was an American educator who contributed to the devel-
    opment of the Japanese education system in the early Meiji period. He especially
    worked for the establishment of Tokyo University and for education for women.
46. Tanaka Fujimaro (1845–1909) joined the Meiji government in 1868 and was placed in
    charge of administering the education system. From 1871 to 1873 he studied the
    education systems in Europe and America as part of the Iwakura Mission. After his
    return to Japan, he became the top-ranking official in the Ministry of Education
    and advocated a decentralized system of education based on the American model.

cal progress was yet another example. It is reported that, in Tokyo, Saigō Takamori said:

> Indiscriminately envying the prosperity of the West without
> considering profit or loss, everything is admired from the
> structure of houses to play things. If we exhaust our resources
> on extravagances, there will be the impoverishment of na-
> tional power, and the people's hearts will be moved to frivol-
> ity. It is as if there is no limit to Japan's resources.

The most amazing example of this trend was Fukuzawa Yukichi,
who argued for the preservation of national customs. Insisting that
it was unsuitable to put low-quality tea in a silver teapot, he criticized the radical Westernization policy of the government. He
raised his voice in criticism of the cosmopolitan belief in the brotherhood of man and the unity of the world.

If you speak of this from the point of view of pure religion, what does the progressiveness or conservatism of the people
have to do with the rise and fall of religion? For the Japanese
people, Christian teachings came from abroad. For this reason
there was a great difference in the degree of development between those periods when foreign culture was welcomed and when
it was not. In this way, the reactionary movement against the West
caused difficulties for the young church.

On 22 September, in the same year as the Mount Hanaoka
incident, Fukuzawa Yukichi harshly criticized Christianity in the
magazine *Katei sōdan*.[47] At the time, Christianity was being blown
along by strong winds, and its sails were filled with future hopes.
His essay was short but his criticism was incisive. First of all, there
were people among the Christian missionaries he called irresponsible fellows who came thousands of miles across the sea to cause
trouble to strangers. He called them begging students who knew
only how to write. They could not look after themselves, but they
inflicted suffering on the spiritual condition of the Japanese
people. They caused trouble to the Japanese people by confusing

47. First published in 1876 by the Keiō College Publishing Company under the supervi-
sion of Fukuzawa, the name of this journal was later changed to the *Minkan zasshi*.

them. Fukuzawa ridiculed them as mouthing morality and trying to enter the Japanese in a registry of God's servants. Even if the brotherhood and the unity of the world were noble ideas, they were nothing more than utopian dreams. His conclusion was that the Japanese people, first of all, should practice independent self-government. Fukuzawa's essay was shorter than that of Yasui Sokken. His position in the intellectual world, however, was not like that of the hermit Yasui. Also, he wrote in a way that anyone could understand. It was a very direct essay. For these reasons, I think it surpassed *An Exposition of Error* in influencing people.

At this point I would like to briefly discuss Fukuzawa Yukichi, the Voltaire of the new Japan. I think he was a great man whose name should be remembered in Japanese intellectual history with gratitude. From the point of view of his opponents, he was a monster who advocated the love of money and depressed the Japanese spirit. He was hated because there was a materialist tendency in his thought. He preached the importance of money for the citizens of new Japan, however, only in the same way that swordsmanship was esteemed in the feudal period. He believed that the basis of the new Japan must be an independent citizenry. For the citizen, the greatest guarantee of independence was money, and it was for this reason that he preached its importance. He understood that one problem was that the thought of old Japan placed importance only on metaphysics and despised empiricism like that of Bacon. For this reason, he advocated investigation in the physical realm. For this reason, he preached Bentham and Mill, applied science and civic morality. In this regard, he represented the needs of the time.

In the things he did, however, he stopped there. He never turned his eyes toward matters other than a this-worldly concern with getting ahead. Also, he looked upon religion as merely an expedient. "If you put your hands together and pray, there are gods and Buddhas." This was his position, and in his attitude to religion he never gave up this way of thinking. It was from this point of view that he viewed the Christians who had just lifted their heads up in the intellectual world. He could not help pouring cold water on them. Judging from his way of thinking, I can guess that he was basically not an ally of the church. The human heart, however, is not satisfied with a this-worldly pursuit of success. Religion has a much deeper root in the human heart than he thought. There is a need in the human heart to respect something higher than what was contained in his attitude toward the world. A section of Japanese youth did not turn to Fukuzawa for this need, but they turned to Niijima Jō. This reactionary movement against the West, however, was also temporarily halted because of the confusion surrounding the Saigō Rebellion.

15

FOUR KINDS OF THOUGHT
AND THE DIVISION OF TALENT

After the Saigō Rebellion finally ended, there was a period of inflation, and the price of rice increased. This increase provided the agricultural class with a surplus. For this reason, there was an outburst of the Popular Rights debate, and the theory of natural rights prospered. It was like spring in the world of public opinion. Christians saw the following four kinds of thought arise and were in a position to evaluate them:

1. The democracy of the French faction: this was represented by scholars who studied French thought.
2. Those influenced by English empiricism and utilitarianism: this group was represented by Keiō College.
3. The conservative reaction: this was represented by the Ministry of Education.
4. The theory of evolution and agnosticism: this was represented by Tokyo University.

Together with the suppression of the Saigō Rebellion, the Conservative Party of Shimazu Hisamitsu and the Liberal Party of the Tosa faction, which had previously surrounded and assaulted the government, ended their attacks. With the rise of public debate, people became agitated. People who had previously helped in government administration gradually left the government and joined the Liberal Party. Those who worked in the government but had supported popular rights separated themselves from the

Popular Rights movement and helped the government's conservative policy. It reached the point where there was a wide gap between the government and the people, and there was a division of talent between the two sides.

Baba Tatsui[48] studied in England and received the support of the government, but after he returned to Japan he joined the Liberal Party. He said of the people at the time:

> On the basis of my ten years' experience, there were many young officials who, while they were in Europe, supported the principles of freedom but who became conservative when they returned to Japan. The reason is not difficult to understand. The young people who go to Europe to study are the children of samurai. The samurai know of no other way of making a living apart from relying on their children. Therefore, when the young people return, the first thing they must do is to look after their family. In order to look after their family, they must have employment. For these young people with new knowledge, there is little work outside the government. For this reason, they cannot help but become government officials. The majority of government officials, however, belonged to the conservative party, so the young people change and become like their colleagues.

Baba's opinion is definitely correct.

The people of Satsuma and Choshu felt the urgent need to win over talented people. For this reason, they threw open their doors and welcomed the talented. Also, they believed in the policy of imitation, so they imported Western culture. They even imported the debate over democratic freedom. They began to feel, however, that encouraging the debate about democracy was more frightening than raising a tiger's cub. They began to wonder whether they had not gone too far. Then the Popular Rights movement flared up, and their hearts were overcome by an extremely conservative reaction. They adopted a policy of repression. A section of the young bureaucracy, which had new knowledge and

---

48. Baba Tatsui (1850–88) studied at Keiō College and made two trips to England in the 1870s to study Western law and politics. He helped organize the Liberal Party but was arrested in 1885 for suspicion of antigovernment activities. After his release in 1886 he went into exile in the United States.

helped administer Japan, unashamedly became the tools of the conservative policy for the reasons Baba stated. People who had warm blood, spirit, and faith, however, could not endure this. At this time, some of them decided to leave the government and live among the people as the people's ally.

16

THE FRENCH FACTION—POLITICAL RIGHTS

We must pay attention to the fact that the majority of the young officials who made this decision had been raised in the study of French ideas and were scholars of French thought. There were people like Numa Morikazu, Ōi Kentarō, and Nakae Chōmin.[49] They were either ejected from the government or else left the government cursing it. They were all scholars of French thought.

In this way, the French faction was the first to separate from the government and become its enemy. They worked to promote natural rights from the beginning. In 1879, members of the Tokyo City Assembly and the Ward Assembly combined and called themselves the Representatives of the Citizens of Tokyo. They invited the emperor to come to Ueno Park. In a public lecture, Numa Morikazu said this was taking the name of the citizens of Tokyo in vain and also ignored the Local Authorities Act. "If this

---

49. Numa Morikazu (1844–90) supported the shogunate during the Meiji Restoration but joined the new government after a short period of imprisonment. In 1879 he resigned his government post because he disagreed with government policies on freedom of speech. He worked as a newspaper publisher and also participated in the establishment of the Liberal Party. Nakae Chōmin (1847–1901) studied Western thought in the late Tokugawa period and was sent to France in 1871 by the Meiji government. He spent three years studying history, politics, and literature and was greatly influenced by French and English liberal thought. After his return in 1874 he served in the bureaucracy for a time but resigned his position in 1877. Subsequently Chōmin became active in politics and wrote extensively. He became known as one of the leading liberals of his day and the principal spokesmen for the radical wing of the Freedom and Popular Rights movement.

important law had a mouth to speak, it would cry out. If it had eyes to see, it would cry tears because of this abuse." It was at this time that Nakae Chōmin produced a translation of Rousseau's *Social Contract* in his *Seiri sōdan* and enthusiastically praised the dignity of the people. The newspaper *Tōyō jiyū shinbun*, with Saionji Kinmochi as president and Matsuda Masahisa and others as writers, discussed the glory of the French Revolution.[50] They praised it as a pure revolution. These activities all show what kind of things the French faction did.

Of course, their thought was very simple. They openly preached the belief that society was nothing more than a social contract, sovereignty lay with the people, and laws were established by the will of the people. For people who were newly awoken to public debate, the simplicity of their theories made them easy to understand. The Liberal Party advanced with the simple theory of natural rights as its banner, and this had a great impact.

They struck at the government with a natural rights spear called "A Petition For the Establishment of a Diet." The government could not help but shrink back from this for it had also grown up in an atmosphere of natural rights. Look at the debate between the petitioners for a National Diet and government officials that took place in the newspapers of the time. Secretary Kanai said, "Rights are received from heaven and government laws cannot prohibit them. These should not be limited at all." Iwakura Tomomi said, "The Japanese people's God-given rights will never be snatched away by the government." It is not difficult to understand the hold natural rights had on people's hearts, for the government did not even try to parry the direct thrust of the natural rights spear.

---

50. Saionji Kinmochi (1849–1940) was one of the most influential politicians in modern Japanese history. Born into an aristocratic family, he served as prime minister twice and held many other important positions. After the Meiji Restoration he studied in France, and after his return became president of the newspaper *Tōyō jiyū shinbun* but was forced to resign by imperial order. Matsuda Masahisa (1845–1914) attended Nishi Amane's private school in Tokyo where he developed an interest in French studies. From 1872 until 1875 he studied in Europe, and after his return he resigned from his government position and participated in the Freedom and Popular Rights movement. In 1881 he joined the staff of the *Tōyō jiyū shinbun*.

17

THE ENGLISH FACTION—EMPIRICISM

Among the people who studied the new knowledge of the West, there were those who looked coldly on the theory of popular rights. These people belonged to the English empiricist-utilitarian group represented by Keiō College and groups who sympathized with it. For the sake of convenience, I would like to call this the English empirical faction. These people spoke of Hume, Buckle, Mill, Bentham, and Gibbon.[51] With regard to science, they favored empiricism; with regard to politics, they favored utilitarianism; and concerning religion, they were sceptical.

I do not doubt that, at the time, the influence of this group was much greater than that of the French Popular Rights faction. Even though for a time the popular rights theory stirred up people's hearts, it was emotional, not scholarly. Even though it satisfied some people because it facilitated discussion, in general terms it did not satisfy the intellectual class, which possessed subtle thought.

Recent history shows that during the period of the Restoration intelligent people in Japan, when they first came in contact with Western civilization, were moved by practical knowledge. In other words, it was the material culture of the West that they were interested in. The first intention of the Restoration government

---

51. David Hume (1711–76), Henry Thomas Buckle (1821–62), Jeremy Bentham (1748–1832), and Edward Gibbon (1737–94) were all prominent British intellectuals whose work was introduced to Japan in the early and mid-Meiji period.

was to import this material culture. This was inevitable, for the Japanese had grown tired of the empty theories of the Sung scholars. One example of this trend was Kurimoto Joun,[52] who went to Paris at the end of the Edo period as the representative of the shogunate. The first things to impress him were the Napoleonic Codes, the law courts, lawyers, the police, gas lights, underground tunnels, zoological and botanical gardens, and museums. Also, the splendor of the opera, and the Grand Hotel, share certificates, steamships, and steam trains. (From *Gyoso tsuiroku*)

The first thoughts the young Japanese politicians Itō, Ōkuma, and Inoue had were for the train between Yokohama and Tokyo and a national telegraph network. They worked at importing Western material civilization. In a letter written in 1872 to Inoue Kowashi,[53] Kido Takayoshi said:

> Last spring, I talked to Toshimichi and he said that in the present situation we should take in as much as possible, and that although in ten or fifteen years problems might appear, people would correct them. It seemed to be a very mature argument but . . .

The Toshimichi referred to in this letter is Ōkubo Toshimichi. Even a conservative like Ōkubo was an extreme reformer with regard to material culture.

I know that even conservative people thought like this. People were amazed by all kinds of material progress. They were surprised by photographs, steam trains, steamships, telescopes, microscopes, and telegraph machines. At the time people simply had new knowledge, and they were in a hurry to use practical tools that could be used in administration. What need was there to discuss the great questions of the universe? People tended to value experience and to respect utility. Dry grass catches fire quickly. It

52. Kurimoto Joun (1822–97) was a shogunate official who worked as naval commissioner and later commissioner of foreign affairs. He attended the Paris Exhibition as a member of the Japanese delegation.
53. Inoue Kowashi (1844–95) joined the Ministry of Justice of the new Meiji government in 1868 and was sent to study in France and Germany in 1872–73. Later he played a significant part in developing the Meiji Constitution, the Imperial Rescript on Education, and other important laws.

was natural that Fukuzawa Yukichi, who inclined toward utilitarianism and scepticism and who poled his boat in the main current
of the time, preached the work of Hume, Bentham, and Mill and
gathered a large number of students. Ono Azusa was a phenomenon of the same sort, for he was trained in the English school
and believed in Benthamism.

Suppose someone has bought a new house. For them the
most urgent business is to get household goods to decorate the
house. In other words, they want to provide material things for
the house. They do not have time to live comfortably in the house
and quietly consider other problems. In the early Meiji period, a
certain group of people were influenced by Western culture and
philosophy. They were sceptical and empirical, and politically they
were utilitarian. This was only because the country of Japan had
moved into a new house.

Even if this group was not the direct enemy of the French
Popular Rights faction, they were not close friends. Rather than
fighting for a utopia like the adherents of the popular rights theory,
they regarded their life's work as practical: trying to improve the
conditions of human life if only by a little. The popular rights
theorists pictured a utopia after the revolution and rushed toward
it. The empirical school had no idealistic vision; they had no utopia; they merely wanted to improve the situation step-by-step.
The people of this faction, and those who had the same ideas,
decided, with much regret, to play up to the government. They
did this because they had seen what the popular rights people
had done. They saw how they had lost out after chasing ideals to
an extreme, and how they were unable to agree easily about
whether to cut themselves off from the government or not. This
group of empirical thinkers, however, was not acceptable to the
government. Even if in thought and feeling they were far from
the popular rights theorists, the fact that they were followers of
new knowledge and wanted reform meant that they were seen as
fellow travelers. Even if in fact this was not the case, seen from
the point of view of a government that dreaded the awakening of
public opinion, it seemed to be like that. After Numa, Nakae,
and Ōi left the government, Ono Azusa, Yano Ryūkei, and Shimada

Saburō[54] remained. The talented graduates of Keiō College, just like university graduates today, entered government service. Seen from the point of view of the conservative element in the government, however, these people were like traitors. The government became increasingly steeped in a conservative atmosphere, and the people became increasingly steeped in a liberal atmosphere. It reached the point where there was no way to harmonize them. The liberal element in the government—Itō Hirobumi, Inoue Kowashi, and Ōkuma Shigenobu—joined together. This changed and became the secret policy of Ōkuma. The Satsuma-Choshu faction panicked, and the situation changed again. On 13 October 1880 there was a coup d'état and the members of the liberal faction were all swept away.[55] There was a standoff between the government and the people.

---

54. Both Yano Ryūkei (1850–1931) and Shimada Saburō (1852–1923) were liberal journalists who joined the government in the 1870s. Along with Ono, they left the government at the time of the political crisis in 1881, when Ōkuma Shigenobu was forced out of the government.

55. In the political crisis of 1881 Ōkuma Shigenobu and his supporters were forced out of the government as a result of factional fighting. The outcome was the reassertion of control of the government by the Satsuma-Choshu faction.

18

THE CONSERVATIVE REACTION AND THE POLICY OF THE GOVERNMENT

There is a poem:

> Deep in the mountains,
> Alone without a friend,
> Faintly in the distance,
> The sound of a woodsman chopping.

When you live deep in the mountains, you cannot help but feel happy when you hear the sound of human footsteps. The government became the enemy of the Liberal Party—the party of reason—and cut itself off from talented, progressive people. In this situation, could the government avoid feeling lonely? As one looks back on those times, it seems that in searching for a friend, the government could find only one. This was the conservative reaction.

While I have divided the intellectual world of the time into the French faction and the English faction, I do not want the reader to overlook the fact that separately there was a conservative trend. In my view, a part of this conservative trend was stimulated by nothing more than a longing for the "good old days." However, if we investigate the basis of this movement and ask what its fundamental origins were, I think we would find more serious causes. I will try to describe these.

(1) The people were not sufficiently satisfied with the new knowledge from the West. The Japanese people were tired of the pantheism of neo-Confucianism. Despite this, there was a need concealed in the bottom of the human heart to regard the source

of morality as an immovable authority. Of course, the Popular Rights theory and the empiricism-scepticism faction could not satisfy this need.

(2) These teachings reflected a materialist tendency and had no power to correct the immorality and bad customs of the time. People recognized this. Looking back at those times, I cannot help but be surprised at the weakness of the power to restrain the immorality of the Japanese people. Just glance at the publications of the time, such as the *Tōkyō shinhanjo ki*, which was published in 1874, and the *Tōkyō shinshi*, which was published continuously from 1874 until 1881 or 1882.[56] Or look at things like the miscellaneous news that was published in various papers. Newspapers described bedroom scenes as they liked; they depicted unbridled love as they liked; and they encouraged sexual promiscuity as they liked. These newspapers scarcely differed from pornography. The government, however, did not ban these things, and the schools did not throw them out the school gate. Young people read them and did not know that reading them was shameful.

According to what I remember, there were many students at the Shizuoka Normal School who read *Tōkyō shinshi*. Also, in 1882 or 1883, when the opening ceremony for the Shizuoka police station was held, I remember seeing prostitutes coming and going from the banquet. In 1879, I read an article in a newspaper that said on 18 June there was a ceremony at the Great Shrine at Hibiya and prostitutes from the Yoshiwara attended. They were met by high- and middle-ranked priests and praised for their faith. I think you can see the trend of the times from this. I had an occasion to go to the Aoyama Cemetery and passed the grave of former Chief of Police Kawaji Toshiyoshi.[57] There was a large stone at the entrance of the grave. On it was carved "Donated by the

56. The *Tōkyō shinhanjo ki* was written by the literary figure Hattori Seiichi (1841–1908) and was a satire on life in Tokyo modeled on Terakado Seiken's *Edo hanjo ki*, which was published in the 1830s. The *Tōkyō shinshi*, which was also published by Hattori, was a satirical journal that began in 1876 and was closed down in 1883 on the grounds that it was offensive to public morals.

57. Kawaji Toshiyoshi (1834–79) was from Satsuma domain, and in 1872 he visited Europe in order to study different police systems. At the time of the controversy over the plan to invade Korea, he established the Tokyo police force in order to maintain order.

Suzaki Bordello." I think this was erected in 1879 or 1880. Would there be such an immoral thing written on the grave of a gentleman today?

One thing is everything. People's debauchery did not just express itself in carnal desire. Let's try to imagine the living conditions in society at that time. There was a lack of order and restraint to an extreme degree.

There was a student swaggering about the streets of Tokyo carrying a Western-style umbrella, and a policeman rebuked him. The student replied, "This is the rule of our movement. I am not harming other pedestrians. Why is it necessary for the police to intervene?" The policeman would not listen, and the student was taken off to the police station. After a while, he saw the policeman smoking. He said "If you have the right to smoke, so do I. Let me!" He did not understand the arguments concerning political rights and freedom. He tried to make his self-indulgent behavior into a principle. This was in 1876, and, in fact, he later became a "gentleman of Meiji Japan."

Not only was there this sort of incident, but it was normal for journalists to libel people in public and not feel any shame at all. One group, the Kyōson Dōshū,[58] whose members had just returned from the West, worried about the extremely harmful effects of this and felt the need for the establishment of a libel law. This was in 1874. People in the university in 1879 or 1880 relate how students at the time did not have uniforms or caps and lived in boarding houses wearing, or not wearing, hemp-soled sandals. Wearing *tabi* and *geta*, they went up and down to the bedrooms or living rooms and even attended lectures.

In this way, many aspects of society were lax, lawless, and without order. I think, however, that this age of self-indulgence and disorder was better than an age in which people are subservient and have no principles. It is better than when people uselessly follow fashion and are hypocritical in the things they do.

58. The Kyōson Dōshū (Coexistence Association) was an organization consisting mainly of students who had returned from overseas and included Baba Tatsui, Kaneko Kentarō, and Ono Azusa. Its objective was to spread liberalism and constitutionalism in Japan.

People at the time did not respect anything because they were sceptical, materialistic, and lacking in belief. Looking back at the way people felt at the time, I know they themselves felt that there was something lacking.

This was the reason the conservative reaction occurred in one part of society. The new learning of the West taught political rights; it taught empiricism; and it taught science. Unlike Buddhism or Confucianism, it did not teach life and it did not teach the way of heaven. The new Western learning taught freedom of thought but had scepticism as its base. Unlike Confucianism or Buddhism, it did not have some moral authority on which to establish human life. Society suffered because the new learning was insufficient to support public morals. It caused anguish because this new learning poured oil on the flames of self-indulgence and immorality. There is always a time, however, when a drunk person sobers up, and there is always a time when a party comes to an end.

I think it should not be regretted that at this time in a part of society there was a revival of Buddhism and Confucianism that taught human behavior, life, and moral authority. This stream of conservatism, however, caught the attention of the government, which was in an isolated position in the intellectual world at the time. There is a saying, "There are Gods who will help you and there are Gods who will abandon you." The government began to look on the conservative reaction with favor, although since the Restoration it had not agreed to participate with the government. If you wait, clear weather will come to the ocean. Before long, the conservative elements became the friend of the government.

In 1882, the *Asano shinbun* wrote: "From now on, the teachings of loyalty, filial piety, and the Confucian virtues are going to appear." It also said:

> When provincial officers go to the capital, they are each admonished by the Imperial Household Ministry and by Tokudai Temple to hold filial piety as a principle and to put the Confucian virtues above all else from now on.

In the same paper in 1883, there was a humorous piece entitled, "The Suffering of Old Confucianists": "The great teacher said,

'The will of heaven revolves.' Recently it has become an objective to revive this passage." The same paper wrote: "In the world recently there has been a yearning for old things. It has become popular to preserve old things."

I do not think this conservative reaction was created through the government's encouragement. I cannot doubt, however, that the government used this conservative reaction and made an ally of the Confucianists, Shinto priests, and rural monks in order to repress the principles of reason and democracy.

19

THE RESULTS OF THE CONSERVATIVE POLICY

In this way the government colluded with the conservative elements to try and restrain the progressive forces. From the point of view of Japanese civilization, however, this was not necessarily a bad thing. Japan was too much in a hurry to imitate foreign things, and there was a need to reflect on the things inside Japan. For many centuries the two religions of Confucianism and Buddhism had sustained the religious needs of the Japanese people. Within these religions existed the principles necessary to form the religious backbone of the people. It was a good policy in keeping with the times to warn people, on the basis of these traditional teachings, against going too far in terms of materialism and imitation. We should not overlook the fact that, even today, there are many people who received a conservative education, who are very vigorous, who have strong physiques, and who are steadfast and loyal. I know that the government's conservatism existed for a reason, but it cannot be denied that this conservatism ran to an extreme and had bad results.

According to my memories of Suruga, as a result of this policy, a large number of young people gave up the English books they had been reading and once again picked up the Chinese classics. The once successful English teachers gradually closed the gates of their schools and moved to Tokyo, where the living was easier. In school education emphasis was placed on the so-called general education of the Ministry of Education of the time. It reached the point where the teaching of basic foreign language was neglected. Teachers of Chinese studies, who had long been hibernating in the country, were once again employed in the elementary schools and middle schools, and they once again occupied the teacher's chair. The young people who had been reading Parley's *History of the World* had to return to the study of the classics. I also forgot the old days when I read *An English Primer* and listened to lectures from the *History of the World*. I went to and from a Chinese school and heard lectures on Confucius and Mencius from an old teacher of the Asaka Gonsai school.[59]

Looking back, I could not bear the humiliation and realized that I must study foreign languages. I talked this over with my relatives and friends. At the time, a middle school teacher said, "Beginning English at your age [I remember I was eighteen at the time], there is no reason to expect you will be able to read an English book freely. What is necessary now is a general education rather than English. I want you to change your objectives." This was the best advice I could have received at the time. Thinking back to that time, however, the population of Shizuoka was about 30,000, and among the children of the samurai, I think you could not point to more than five young people who, like my friends and me, were studying English. Of course, it goes without saying that this was only my experience. If you understand that the fall of a leaf means that autumn has come, then you can understand that the results of the government's conservative policy was to make young people neglect the study of foreign language and to make many of them uselessly read worn-out old books.

59. Asaka Gonsai (1791–1861) was a Confucian scholar of the late Tokugawa period.

20

The Attitude of Christians

Christians became involved in these intellectual debates and had various experiences. At the time they were treated in a way similar to Popular Rights activists. Of course, when the political debate arose, there was a natural tendency for some of them to ally themselves with reason and democracy. The reasons are not difficult to understand. Christianity was close to the Western intellectual world, and reason and democracy were the products of that world. This is the first reason they were close. Among the influential people in the church, people like Niijima Jō had breathed the air of freedom and in his heart he believed in democracy. Most of the foreign missionaries, too, had been raised in the midst of political freedom. This is the second reason they were close. I have already described how most Christians were the children of the defeated or of people who had passed through an environment similar to that of the defeated. The majority of the people who advocated reason and democracy tended to come from the dissatisfied element in society. There was a natural tendency for people from this kind of environment to feel sympathy for one another. This was the third reason they were close. These, however, were only secondary reasons.

The main reason was that the government became attached to the conservative reaction and became imbued with the mood of that environment. Christianity was not the enemy of the government. The government's policy, however, poured oil on the flames of the conservative reaction. Some people in the conservative reaction confused Christians with those who advocated reason and democracy. Even if they knew that politics and religion were not the same, they attacked Christianity in order to injure the opposing party. This caused Christians to quickly show sympathy for the Liberal Party, and it caused the Liberal Party to draw close to Christians. This was the main reason the Liberal Party and the Christians drew close to each other.

According to Honda Yōichi, in 1874 he returned to Hirosaki and became a teacher at Tōō College, which had been built by his domain. The fact that he was a Christian caused trouble twice. The first time was in 1876 or 1877, when it became known that there was interference from Iwakura Tomomi. At this time, through some kind of an excuse, he did not have to give up teaching. The second instance of interference was in 1882 or 1883. The Ministry of Education communicated to the Imperial Household Department, and Kaieda Nobuyashi,[60] the steward of the Konoe family, contacted the former domain lord. There is a story that the Konoe family and the Tsugaru were closely related and that their connections were deep. The excuse for intervention was that it was not suitable for a person in the Liberal Party or a Christian to be employed by a school. Honda said, "Even if the government did not put the main emphasis on their dislike of my being in the Liberal Party, I was caught because I was a Christian. At that time, if I had not left, it would have affected the fate of the school, so I had no choice but to leave Tō College." I think this explains the position of most Christians at the time.

There was a report that on 10 March 1882, in Kofu, the head of the Liberal Party, Itagaki Taisuke, publicly showed sympathy for Christians by saying Buddhism, Shintoism, and Confucianism were obstacles to the advancement of the country. If you think about this, you can understand that at that time a part of the Liberal Party, which represented the Popular Rights movement, had enough sympathy for Christianity to give it encouragement.

---

60. Kaieda Nobuyashi (1832–1906) was from Kagoshima and actively participated in the Meiji Restoration. Subsequently, he held a variety of different administrative positions in the new government.

21

THE UNIVERSITY MOVEMENT AND THE
THEORY OF EVOLUTION AND AGNOSTICISM

The direct opponent of Christianity at the time, however, was not the Buddhist and Confucian reaction. Reactionary groups, even if they did not like Christianity, occurred in response to the scepticism and self-indulgence of the times, just as Christianity did. Direct theoretical opposition to Christianity came from the so-called English empirical school. Tokyo University, which had long been a center of influence, suddenly arose and became active, encouraging the idea of agnosticism and the theory of evolution. A new movement occurred in the spiritual world, and Christians came to feel that a new enemy had come into being. After 1880 or 1881, the university contributed two kinds of activities to the Japanese spiritual world. One was the theory of evolution introduced by Professor Morse.[61] The other was Katō Hiroyuki's denial of political rights.

At that time, the Japanese intellectual world was usually ten or more years behind the Western intellectual world since Japan had newly awoken to world civilization. For example, Fukuzawa Yukichi spoke about people like Mill and Bentham, but they were figures in the history of philosophy and did not deal with contemporary problems. Their names, however, stirred up a new emotion in Japan, and their work was of sufficient novelty to arouse

---

61. Edward Morse (1838–1925) was an American zoologist who traveled to Japan in 1877 to study Pacific brachiopods. Until he returned to the United States in 1879, he taught at Tokyo University and organized its zoology department.

new intellectual activity. Even though for the English the empiricism and utilitarianism they advocated were well known, for the Japanese they were something new. They gave rise to a special kind of emotion because they were something fresh. In reality, it was the same with the theory of evolution and agnosticism in Tokyo University. Darwin's *On the Origin of Species* appeared in 1859, and Spencer appeared as an advocate of agnosticism in the Keiō period (1865–67) or at the beginning of the Meiji period. In the intellectual world, Tokyo University, however, began to introduce and teach these works only in about 1880 or 1881.

I remember something from this time very clearly. Professor Morse, who was a teacher at Tokyo University, gave lectures about the theory of evolution at various places, such as the Ibu Village Hall. He explained that people had evolved from animals resembling monkeys. In most cases his translator was Professor Kikuchi Dairoku.[62] In writing the history of the theory of evolution in Japan, the names of Morse and Kikuchi Dairoku must not be forgotten. As a result of the labor of these two men, *On the Origin of Species* was introduced to Japan even though it was nothing special in the West.

What invited public attention, however, was the activity of Katō Hiroyuki, the president of the university. On the basis of the theory of evolution, he attacked the theory of natural rights. He became the president of the university in July 1881. In the past, he had preached freedom and democracy, as evidenced by his works *A New Theory on the National Polity*, and *An Outline of Practical Politics*. At the time of his becoming the president of the university, he claimed that his previous advocacy of democracy was the result of youthful indiscretion. His early works went out of print, and at the end of the following year, his new position became clear through his new book entitled *A New Theory of Human Rights*. This was a small book of no more than one hundred pages, with ten lines to the page and fifty characters to the line.

---

62. Kikuchi Dairoku (1855–1917) was a mathematician and educational administrator who devoted himself to the introduction of Western mathematics to Japan. He studied mathematics and physics at Cambridge University for about ten years.

Katō applied the theory of evolution to the study of politics, and under the pretext of being an advocate of human rights, he directly attacked the theory of natural rights. This book shocked the intellectual world.

In order to provide an outline of the argument contained in *A New Theory of Human Rights*, I will quote several paragraphs:

> We humans, just like plants and animals, receive the hereditary influence of our parents and ancestors in our physical and psychological dispositions. Also, there are differences among us because our physical and psychological dispositions change under the influence of the countless number of things we encounter while we are alive. For this reason, there is unceasing competition among people. In this competition, however, the superior are always victorious, and they oppress the inferior. In other words, a natural weeding-out process comes into being. This also cannot be avoided. This is the so-called survival of the fittest. If you look at this, you must understand that the mechanism of the survival of the fittest, which is a law controlling all things, not just in the animal and plant world, but in the human world, is born of necessity. This mechanism of the survival of the fittest is a principle born of necessity in our human society. If you doubt this, then it is very clear that you must believe a fallacious argument such as the theory of natural rights, which holds that while people are all born individually, we all have fixed, equal rights of self-government and freedom.
>
> If you wish to have a stable society, then there must be a technique put into practice to prevent the self-indulgence of the superior people who have exclusive power over the masses. If this is not done, then there will merely be the struggle for survival among the people, and the superior individuals will overpower inferior individuals. As a consequence, there will not be a stable society. If this is done, however, the most superior person of all will use his power to implement a policy prohibiting the self-indulgence of the superiors among the people. What other techniques need to be employed? This is all. By assigning rights and responsibilities to all the people, the self-indulgence of the superior people will be prohibited. If somebody kills a person without reason, cheats somebody of their property, or even if somebody insults another person, the superior person, that is, the person with absolute power, will put the criminal to death, banish him, or will use another method to punish him. Also, punishing someone will greatly help to prevent future criminal disputes. Therefore, the

>people will have the responsibility to mutually prevent in-
jury to other people's lives, property, and honor, and they will
also have the right to prevent such injury. This is the reason
rights first came into being, and they depend on the ruler
who holds absolute power, in other words, the most superior
person.

In this way, on the basis of heredity Katō denied the existence of human rights. So-called rights were nothing more than things established for the convenience of the strong.

In the 17th century, Thomas Hobbes wrote *Leviathan*, a book that was to become quite famous.[63] In this book it is said that the natural condition of man was that of warfare. Various people want various things and have a need for various things. In order to try to escape from this state of warfare, the most important thing was for people to respect one authority and be submissive to it. Societies came into existence because of this necessity. There was no such thing as righteousness before societies came into existence. Society was created out of expediency. He explained that power surpasses rights. It was not only Hobbes who thought this way. In the Kyōhō era (1716–35), Ogyū Sorai also asserted that the "Way of Man" was not ordained by heaven but was something established by the sages for the safety of the people.

In history, there is no phenomenon that exists in isolation. What Katō presented to the world as his own new theory was merely the revival of Hobbes and Sorai in the disguise of the theory of evolution. Morality and the laws that control people are simply conveniences to maintain society. Katō could not help but arouse public opinion, however, because he used the theory of evolution, which was a new idea in Japan, as a weapon in this debate. Also, the debate was a very fundamental one that concerned the basis of social organization.

In this way, Tokyo University, through Morse, taught the idea of the descent of man; through Katō, it taught denial of the

---

63. Thomas Hobbes (1588–1679) was an English philosopher who emphasized the practical importance of knowledge. He believed that human beings were essentially
   selfish, and in *Leviathan* (1651) he argued that it was necessary for there to be a
   supreme ruler so as to mitigate the effects of individual selfishness and maintain
   social order.

existence of natural rights; and through the students of Toyama Masakazu,[64] it preached the philosophy of Spencer. In other words, the university taught that people could know only phenomena. People could not directly confront the essential nature of the universe, and the nature of things themselves was unknowable. The university also asserted that the real origin of things was unknowable.

Through this kind of activity, Tokyo University had a tremendous influence in arousing a new consciousness in the world at a time when people were growing tired of the French political rights theory and British empiricism. Recalling that time, I cannot help but imagine the tremendous influence the university actually had on the Japanese intellectual world. I recall that those intellectual waves even reached the small group of young men who were my friends in Shizuoka, where I was then living. I remember our youth group even having a debate and discussion about the agnosticism that was topical at the time. I had earlier inclined toward a belief in God, but I fell into a state of doubt because of the influence of these ideas. Also, at that time I loved to read *A New Theory of Human Rights*, and I believed the ideas it contained. Among my friends of that time there was one who was studying law. He read Boissonade's *Lectures on Customary Law*, and he introduced it to me.[65] At the time, I recoiled from this and said, "Customary law? Do you believe in natural law? Law is merely established by the powerful for convenience. I do not believe that we should have customary law, so I cannot read this honestly." We did not fear heaven and we did not believe in God. We had fallen into the dangerous situation of thinking law was a promise among men and nothing more than a temporary convenience. This also, however, was nothing more than the consequences of the influence of Morse, Katō, and Toyama.

---

64. Toyama Masakazu (1848–1900) was the first Japanese Professor of Philosophy and Sociology at Tokyo University. He later became president of the university and also served as education minister in 1898. As a believer in the Spencerian theory of cultural evolution, he advocated replacing the Japanese script with the roman alphabet.

65. Gustave Emil Boissonade de Fontarabie (1825–1910) was a French legal scholar who came to Japan in 1873 to provide legal advice to the Meiji government.

22

TOKYO UNIVERSITY AGAINST THE CHRISTIAN CHURCH

The teachings of Tokyo University, however, were insufficient to truly satisfy the human heart. No matter what the time, people are always people. If they cannot achieve some firm foundation of belief in their hearts, they will have a great and unceasing need. For human beings, a sense of morality is not a temporary expediency. For this reason, out of Sorai's theory of expediency came an inevitable return to the teachings of Zhu Xi by the "Three Scholars of the Kansei Period." In the Zhu Xi school of thought, the problem of human life is an endless link of causes, and a sense of morality is a timeless pledge. Even though Hobbes's theory of resistance was dominant for a while, the English could not help but return to the thought of John Locke.[66] This was because Locke's sense of morality was linked to the idea of God. The same cause cannot help but produce the same result.

I can give as an example my own feelings as a young person at the time. I greatly respected *A New Theory of Human Rights*, and I greatly admired the idea of agnosticism. In my heart I had contempt for the idea of a social contract. At the same time, however, I could not help but feel dissatisfied in my inner heart. I had given up the teachings of Confucius. I could not forget, however,

66. John Locke (1632–1704) was an English philosopher who was a strong advocate of religious freedom. He believed that human understanding is not commensurate with reality and that knowledge must therefore be supplemented by religious faith. He also opposed the idea of the divine right of kings and believed the state rested on a contract between ruler and ruled that involved reciprocal obligations.

the satisfaction I derived from Confucianism, which had as its immutable foundation a sense of morality that unified the Way of Heaven with the Way of Man. I had the feeling that the teachings of the university group had freed me from my old beliefs. Liberation, however, is not peace of mind. In fact, the teachings of the university faction had caused me to fall into a dark valley, and there was no way I could conceive of to try to resolve this situation. I could not help but grope toward the light. Were these my feelings alone? Or, did a certain number of the young people of the time suffer from a spiritual dilemma concerning the problem of human life and have the same feelings as myself?

In the intellectual world at that time there was no authority. There was no unity. There was confusion. It was like the fighting among local warlords that produced no result. One school of thought fought with another school of thought. They in turn fought with another school of thought. It was like an age of great heroes and warriors.

It was at this time that I saw the Christians struggle the hardest. There was a burst of energy caused by Niijima Jō's Dōshisha College in Kyoto. Also, the so-called Kumamoto Band of young people, who had pledged together on Mount Hanaoka, threw themselves into the fray. The elders in these groups soon dispersed in different directions and extended the lines of missionary work.

In Tokyo, intellectuals within the church combined to publish *Rikugō zasshi.*[67] As a weapon in the spiritual world, this became more and more powerful. I heard that at the same time that *Rikugō zasshi* was first published, Christians in Tokyo planned to open a large, open-air church at Suribachiyama in Ueno as a part of a more aggressive movement. Tsuda Sen,[68] an elder in the church, acted as a representative and asked the opinion of Itō Hiro-

---

67. *Rikugō zasshi* (Cosmos) was established in 1880 as the journal of the YMCA. As a journal that dealt not only with religious matters but also with the arts, education, society, and politics, it was very influential. Contributors included leading Christian intellectuals of the time, such as Ebina Danjō, Uchimura Kanzō, and Kozaki Hiromichi.

68. Tsuda Sen (1837–1908) was a leading agricultural writer of the Meiji period who had visited the United States and Europe in 1867 as a part of the government mission that had included Fukuzawa Yukichi.

bumi, the Minister of the Interior. Itō replied that it was permissible, and thus preparations were happily begun. The police feared, however, that if a large, open-air church were permitted, then the Liberal Party would also be permitted to do something similar. Finally, it reached the stage where permission was not given, and the church had to give up the plan. As a result, instead of this, they held a large lecture meeting at the Seiyokan in Ueno.

Beginning with Dōshisha, the so-called missionary schools established themselves and worked to educate the fighters necessary for the spiritual war. The *Rikugō zasshi* became increasingly vigorous and fought with sceptics, empiricists, utilitarians, and even more the university faction. At the time, *Rikugō zasshi* was a rarity in the literary world, and it never succumbed to weakness. Looking at the traces of the strong fight it put up against the university, I cannot help but be moved by its brave editors. At first, they argued that the theory of evolution did not have complete scholarly authority. In this regard Dr. Faulds,[69] president of Tsukiji Hospital, was a worthy opponent of Morse. When Morse raised a point, Faulds would raise the same point. He refuted Morse by arguing that the theory of evolution was not something we necessarily had to believe in.

Faulds realized, however, that he could not fight against the theory of evolution like that, and thus he changed his method of argument and claimed that the theory of evolution was not incompatible with a belief in God. Progressing from there, he argued that experience showed that the theory of evolution came from the great intellect of God. He said that the discoveries of Copernicus, the empiricism of Bacon, and the new research methods of science were once seen as trying to destroy the fundamentals of Christian belief. For this reason the church had been very fearful. In reality, however, this view was a fallacy that had merely tarnished the name of faith. In fact, science is nothing but praise of the glory of God. He argued that the theory of evolution within the Christian church was simply another example of this. He did

---

69. Henry Faulds (1843–1930) was a Scottish medical missionary and an amateur scientist. He lived in Japan from 1874 until 1886.

not think that the theory of evolution was strong enough to destroy the Christian faith. Those who argued for spiritualism tried to go back to the origin of the real universe, and this was a reaction against empiricism. This was nothing more than a manifestation of mankind's desire to search out God. Whenever I see copies of the *Rikugō zasshi* of that time, I cannot avoid being moved by the tremendous spirit it had.

At that time, the Christian church was quiet, but it was advancing in firm steps. Moreover, the quiet political conditions after 1884 or 1885 were suitable for the advance of Christianity.

23

THE RISE OF WESTERNISM

Treaty revision had troubled the minds of our political leaders for a long time. About 1883 or 1884, public opinion once again turned toward this problem. In 1887, when it looked as though the Inoue plan would be successful, popular emotion concerning this issue reached a peak. If you look at this simply as a political problem, it has no connection with intellectual history. We cannot doubt that the policy of the government at the time, however, was to enact laws in accordance with Western principles, encourage the study of foreign languages, and encourage contact between Japanese and non-Japanese in order to achieve a smooth conclusion to the revision plan. As much as possible, the government wished to dress up the Japanese as Westerners, and the result of this was that the so-called Westernization policy came into being.

From the beginning people outside the government welcomed Western-style education, supported this trend, and called for the Westernization of Japan. We can see this change of thought in all kinds of phenomena. For example, the number of people going abroad increased. Many politicians, their supporters, scholars, and military men undertook world sightseeing tours. Groups arose like the Roman Script Society and the Theatre Reform Society. There were calls for all kind of reforms, such as reform of the writing system; unification of the spoken and written language; reform of novels; reform of art; and reform of food, clothing, and housing. This reached an extreme with those who called for intermarriage with Westerners in order to reform human beings. Everything in Japan was to be changed in terms of both spirit and form. From the point of view of law, there was the desire to make Japan a part of the so-called Western international group.

I remember visiting a teacher of Western studies in Suruga at that time. When I asked him what we should do with regard to Japanese manners and customs, he replied in the following way: "I advocate the complete imitation of the West. With regard to architecture, with regard to decoration, and with regard to literature. I want to learn from the West." Even though I was not convinced by the comments of this teacher, I did not think that a person who had an attitude like this had lost all common sense. At the time, it was not simply this one teacher who thought like that.

I remember the plots of many popular novels at the time. A man and woman would fall in love freely; the main characters in the book would use English and French words; their lifestyles were those of Western ladies and gentlemen; and the climax of their love would end with their marriage in a Christian church. In addition, the literary style used by the authors completely departed from the characteristic Japanese style. They used a translated Western literary style and employed such symbols as ! ? = and so on. In this way the study of English became popular. There was the sudden development of girls' schools, and there were many students at coeducational mission schools. It is not surprising that Christianity also increased in vitality.

Tokyo University's Toyama Masakazu, who had introduced Spencer's thought to Japan, changed his thinking. In contrast to his former sarcastic criticism of Christianity, he expressed goodwill toward it. A political insider, Foreign Minister Inoue Kowashi, often showed respect to important people among the Christian missionaries, inviting them to his mansion and thus tacitly showing favor to them. For Christians, this situation was similar to a nightingale coming out of a stony ravine and singing triumphantly as it sits among luxurious foliage. They could see only the broad prospects ahead. They were like Moses seeing the promised land open up before his eyes. Many young people were moved by this intellectual current, and they gathered at the door of the church of their own will. There were more people at a meeting of the Christian church than at a meeting of a political party. "Let's make Japan a Christian country. The fields are turning golden, now is the time to harvest." At the time, all Christians felt like this. Christians were the children of good fortune with great expectations.

Finally, however, the Inoue plan failed. The Westernization policy, which had been artificially brought about, was cynically buried. The interest that had grown up in Western scholarship and culture, however, did not suddenly decline due to the failure of the government's policy. At first, the intellectual world had fallen into the hands of the conservatives. Following this, there had been a move in the direction of the new Western studies. After this, however, people wished to preserve old things. Then suddenly there had been the imitation of Western styles. This trend was based on the encouragement of the government, which was eager to revise the treaties. The people whose minds had been greatly awoken by Western civilization, however, did not wish for an immediate change of pace because of a stumble in the government's policy. Therefore, even though, as a result of the humiliating defeat of the Inoue plan, common people cursed the frivolity of a fancy dress ball, intellectuals still advocated the renewal of Japan, the building of a new Japan, and the baptism of Japan in nineteenth-century culture. The fact that this kind of thought controlled the hearts of the Japanese people was symbolized by two magazines: Tokutomi Sohō's[70] *Kokumin no tomo* and Iwamoto Yoshiharu's[71] *Jogaku zasshi*. I would like to briefly discuss these two magazines.

70. Tokutomi Sohō (1863–1957) was born in Kumamoto and was a member of the Kumamoto Band. He later studied at Dōshisha College with Niijima Jō before moving to Tokyo where he established Min'yūsha, a company that published the journal *Kokumin no tomo*.

71. Iwamoto Yoshiharu (1863–1942) was born in Hyōgo Prefecture and became a Christian under the influence of Tsuda Sen. He became interested in women's rights and education and advocated economic independence for women as well as the abolition of prostitution. He founded the *Jogaku zasshi* (Journal of Women's Study) with Kondō Kenzō.

24

THE *KOKUMIN NO TOMO* AND *JOGAKU ZASSHI*

In a small corner of Kyushu, in the eastern suburbs of Kumamoto, there was a small village school called Ōe College. This was nothing more than a small group of students. The old teacher who was the center of the school was called Tokutomi Kisui, and he was a follower of the Shōnan school of practical learning. For the students, however, the spiritual leader was really his eldest son, Tokutomi Sohō. The school was open from 1882 until 1886, when Sohō was a young man of twenty to twenty-four. He was, however, a gifted person from the Niijima school who politically favored freedom and had an interest in things Western. At the time he did not claim to be an orthodox Christian, but he was a member of the Kumamoto Band. Not only was he a beloved disciple of Niijima Jō, but most of his friends were Christians. Therefore, if one had to define which group of people he belonged to on the basis of his thought, one would have to view him as a Christian.

The reader must recall that Kumamoto at that time was a world of conservative groups, such as the Shimeikai school and Sasa Tomofusa's Seiseikō school.[72] The war cries of state rights, conservatism, and theocracy could be clearly heard all around Ōe College. Ōe College had objects thrown at it in the middle of the night by hooligans from the opposition party. If the people who

---

72. The Shimeikai (1881–84) was a political group in Kumamoto established to oppose the Freedom and Popular Rights movement. The Seiseiko was a school founded by the Shimeikai to propagate its ideas.

passed through the school gate were not seen as traitors, they were at least embryonic traitors.

But look! A believer in progress grew up among these conservative surroundings. He came out of this environment and climbed up onto the literary stage in Tokyo. On 15 February 1887, the first issue of the *Kokumin no tomo* appeared and was met by great applause. Thanks to popular support it became successful.

Unfortunately, I do not know the history of Iwamoto Yoshiharu's *Jogaku zasshi* as well as I know that of the *Kokumin no tomo*. It appeared about the same time as the *Kokumin no tomo*, boldly preaching Christianity and encouraging an interest in the West. The fact that these two magazines had a large number of readers shows that they were two clear symbols through which we can understand the intellectual current of the time.

I respect Tokutomi's genius and I recognize that Iwamoto was a brilliant person. It would be a mistake, however, to attribute the success of these magazines simply to the talent of individuals. The reason the Japanese people loved these two men and regarded them as two jewels in the literary world was not that they were geniuses but that they met the requirements of the time. This must be recognized by anyone who looks dispassionately at the intellectual world of the time. I think that the success of these two magazines is proof that Japan had a need for new principles and new beliefs. At the same time, it is proof that Christianity was looked on with favor by the world.

25

THE MOVEMENT AT DŌSHISHA COLLEGE

At the time when the Christian church was full of hope, Niijima Jō began the movement to establish Dōshisha College. In fact, this was an extremely bold plan by Christians. Up until this time only three groups had put a great deal of effort into the Japanese educational world. These were the government schools belonging to Tokyo University or the Ministry of Education, Count Ōkuma's Senmon Gakkō, and Fukuzawa Yukichi's Keiō College. These three groups were the center of activity, and, indeed, society was divided among the three of them. In spite of the fact that Christians had become involved with "mission schools" in various places, their efforts had been very weak, and they could not compare with the other three groups. Now they took a great step forward, and immediately they wished to mark out a kingdom in the Japanese educational world based on Christian education.

From the beginning, Niijima Jō had a deep and broad interest in spiritual education. He was a missionary, but he did not wish to divide education and missionary work into two parts. Education and missions were two aspects of spiritual training. Above all else, he deeply believed that education was the most urgent necessity for Japan. He had lived in a free country for a long time, and his understanding of the need to respect freedom and independence was much higher than that of the average Japanese. When he was in America and met the first envoys of new Japan, Iwakura, Ōkubo, and Kido, he did not follow the Japanese custom of bowing before them but wished to use an American-style democratic greeting. Not only that, but he made it publicly known that he did not want to be treated in the same way as the twelve Japanese students studying in America at the government's expense. This was because he believed himself to be an independent person raised in a free country.

As a person Niijima Jō was conservative. He tended to restrain his emotions. He was not very open and did not arouse young people, nor was he admired by young people. He was not open like Ogyū Sorai, and he was not fearless like Nichiren.[73] In other words, he was a person who restrained his own personality and did not show it to the outside. For this reason, he never had the kind of personality that lay people loved. Not only was he misunderstood by people at the time, but even Christians were suspicious of his thoughts. Beneath this withdrawn, restrained, and closed outer garment, however, was an intimidating seriousness. He was not a good-natured person who could make friends anywhere, but for his few friends he had an honest and passionate love. With this kind of honesty he was a believer in democracy. Having this kind of personality, he could not close his eyes to the weaknesses of the Japanese education system into which the government scholars had put their efforts. According to his view, the Japanese government's education system had some merits. Japan's Imperial University had turned out a number of talented people. A child, however, lives in its mother's womb, and just as the mother's womb has a connection with the nature of the child, so the products of government schools could not avoid the characteristics of bureaucratic scholarship. Clever private secretaries and skilled technicians were produced. Lawyers were produced who could analyze the minute details of law. These people, however, were merely technicians and bureaucrats. You could not expect really talented people or people with an unbending character to come out of such a system. "First of all, let's liberate education from the hands of government officials." This is what he deeply believed.

---

73. Nichiren (1222–82) was a Buddhist monk who founded the Nichiren sect of Buddhism (also known as the Hokke or Lotus sect) in the Kamakura period.

Concerning this point, neither the Senmon Gakkō faction nor the Keiō College faction would object to this view. Niijima Jō, however, while agreeing with those at the Senmon Gakkō and Keiō College on this point, wished to enshrine education on a much higher platform than they did. He was not satisfied simply to make a person useful in the present world.

A writer in the *Kokumin no tomo* explained this point well. Through his principles of education, Niijima Jō wished to endow people with a "world of noble lifestyles." For example, a person of religion was not someone who simply prayed but was also someone who was righteous in the eyes of God. A politician should not stop at being a clever politician, but should also love people and the country. A literary person should not only be skilled in writing but should also be sincere and love justice and truth. As for people, they should not just work industriously for food and clothing. They should also be able to have a noble and refined lifestyle in terms of their conduct, their nature, and their character. These were his principles of education.

On the basis of these principles, Niijima Jō had a plan to establish the so-called Dōshisha College. In 1885 he returned to the United States, his second home, and appealed to philanthropists to donate money. He returned to Japan, and in 1888 he made public a prospectus for establishment of the college. Sparing no effort in his activities, he left Kyoto and went to Tokyo.

At that time, he had a serious nervous illness, and people feared that his death was not far away. With his brave spirit, however, he did not lie down on a sick bed but acted as if he were unaware that death's hand was about to seize him. The cold was a great danger to his nervous condition, but he went from Kyoto to Tokyo at a time of freezing cold. He entered Ueno at a time of freezing cold, but he wished to go on to Fukushima. He gave up the idea of this trip because of a talk with a passerby, and he returned from Ueno to Tokyo again. If he had gone on, surely his bones would be buried beyond the Shirakawa barrier. When the winds blow up, the clouds fly. In the area of spiritual education, he was like a typhoon.

Even among the part of society that until then had despised the efforts of the Christian church, there was some surprise that it had reached this level. Tokyo University's Toyama Masakazu, a true child of Edo and a person full of conceit, seeing this situation, publicized the advantages of education at the Imperial University and tried to resist this development. At the time, however, Christianity was welcomed by the progressive people in Japan. There were many who expressed support for Niijima Jō's work, and there were many financial contributions.

26

Weaknesses in the Work of Niijima Jō

I would like to try to evaluate the work of Niijima Jō. Unfortunately, he died in midlife, and thus we cannot know what would have been the results of his efforts. In terms of modern Japanese history, however, he made such a valuable contribution that we must have sympathy for him as a person. To speak honestly, however, at a basic level Niijima's work had one great fault: he went along with the things the foreign missionaries did. As I wrote in my review of Davis's book, *The Life of Niijima Jō*:

> In Japan there are any number of devout people who, because they have gone along with the things the foreign missionaries have done, have needlessly had their spiritual energy ground down and strangely accepted responsibility for the mistakes of others. I cannot endure the grief of seeing so many lose their intellectual energy. In this book, the honest Davis records how from the beginning of Dōshisha College, because of certain foreign missionaries, there was suspicion, wasted effort, obstruction, and interference. Niijima also criticized the American Missionary Society, saying that many talented young people had become disillusioned with Dōshisha because the foreign teachers went to excess in teaching the Bible and were negligent in the teaching of arts and science. They did not know about the conditions in Japan, and Niijima criticized them for not training Japanese missionaries but seeking the assistance of missionaries from their own country. He knew that their troublesome interference was not right. If from the beginning he had been in Kyoto by himself with the common people, he would have been in an environment

where he could have done what he wanted. If he had possessed the consciousness of a truly independent missionary, I believe his influence would have been great. This is merely to say what he had the potential to do. From the time he got money from Mr. Hardy, Niijima's fate was to be the prisoner of the Foreign Missionary Society. That he never separated from the society was largely fate. Am I being too harsh in my opinion? I find only joy in independence. I find joy in honest belief. I wish to weep because a great spirit suffered in the chains of the Foreign Missionary Society.

The idea of Dōshisha was good, but Dōshisha was within the range of influence of the foreign missionaries. It was thus not a school that had true independence and freedom. Niijima Jō freed education from the hands of the government officials, but he put it into the hands of the missionaries. This was a change only in form, not substance. This was just buying one kind of freedom by selling another. In this regard, I see only Fukuzawa Yukichi as having surpassed all others. The reason is that he did not depend on anybody but independently built up his educational work.

27

THEOLOGICAL DISPUTES I

The Christian church in Japan reached the peak of its success at about the time of the movement to establish Dōshisha College. For the Christian church after this, on the one hand there was repression from the outside because of the conservative reaction, and, on the other hand, there was a weakening within the church because of theological disputes. From that time on, for about twenty years, no growth could be seen in the church.

First, I would like to talk about the theological disputes.

Here the backwardness of the Japanese intellectual world can be clearly seen. The idea of the theory of evolution was first heard among the Japanese people in about 1880 or 1881. This had no direct connection with the publication of Darwin's *On the Origin of Species*, which had first appeared about twenty years before, in 1859. The Japanese theological world lagged far behind the theological world of the West. Strauss's *Life of Christ* was published in 1835. Baur was the founder of the Tübingen school, and his book, *Studies on the Life of Mark*, was published in 1851. He died in 1860.[74] Theological students in Japan could not afford to overlook this new critical and historical study if they wished to be

---

74. The Tübingen school (named after a university in Germany) is used to refer to a group of scholars that revolutionized biblical studies in the middle of the 19th century. The head of the school was Ferdinand Christian Baur (1792–1860), but the beginnings of the school itself is dated from the publication of the *Life of Jesus* (1835) by Baur's former student, David Friedrick Strauss (1808–74).

well informed about knowledge from all over the world, for it had caused great waves in the theological world.

Strangely, however, scholars who were connected with the Christian church knew nothing of the Higher Criticism school until thirty years after Baur's death. The foreign missionaries taught the old mold-encrusted theology, and most of them did not doubt it. I know that around 1889 there was not one influential missionary in Japan who knew the name of Baur and Strauss. Even if this was just by chance, it is one piece of evidence that Christian theology was in its infancy in Japan. With regard to this point, the Christian church of the time did not have the right to ridicule the Imperial University of the day.

Once the human heart awakens, however, it does not go back to sleep again. From about 1884 or 1885 there appeared Christians who paid attention to the new theology. There began a groping toward new knowledge that would shake the foundations of Christianity. In this regard, Yano Ryūkei's *Fukuchi shinbun* advocated Unitarianism.[75] The clergyman Spinner came to Japan from the German Evangelical Protestant Missionary Society, which was steeped in the Tübingen school of thought.[76] Also, in the spring of 1888, the American Unitarian Knapp came to Japan and attended meetings in various places and explained his beliefs. In autumn, Mr. and Mrs. Schmiedel of the German Evangelical Protestant Missionary Society came. There was also the appearance of the German New Evangelical Society. In 1890 the magazine *Unitarian* was published to advocate Unitarian principles. The magazine *Shinri* also appeared, with the aim of spreading the concepts associated with the Higher Criticism of the Tübingen school. In addition, the "Universalist" missionary Perin[77] came to Japan.

---

75. Unitarianism was introduced to Japan in 1887 with the arrival of Arthur May Knapp of the American Unitarian Association.
76. The Evangelical Protestant Missionary Society (Der allgemeine evangelisch protestantische missionsverein), which was founded in 1884, was based in Germany and Switzerland. The society sent the missionary Wilfred Spinner to Japan in 1885, and he was followed by Otto Schmiedel in 1887. The journal *Shinri* appeared in 1889.
77. The first mission sent by the Universalist General Convention of America under the leadership of George L. Perin arrived in Japan in 1890.

In this way, Christians in Japan also came to hear about the teachings of the Unitarians and Universalists.

Until that time, however, discussions about Christianity had been mainly philosophical and had not been sufficient to shake the faith of the so-called orthodox church. The Unitarians used philosophy as a weapon, and the orthodox church fought with them in the same way they had fought with the philosophy of Mill and Spencer. Only when it came to the Tübingen school, represented by the German Evangelical Protestant Missionary Society, was there a force sufficiently strong to affect people emotionally. No one seemed to know a reason, however, why this should be resisted.

The weapon of this group was research on the Old and New Testament based on scientific and historical criticism. Until then, when they had encountered the criticism of philosophers, Christians had argued that Christ was a historical person and Christianity was the product of history. They argued that the Bible was trustworthy as a historical document. Even philosophers could not shake historical fact. The Tübingen school, however, changed direction and made scientific inquiry a part of the historical credibility of Christianity. This was to turn the tables, to attack our bastion, and wave our sword. Japanese Christians could not help but become confused in the face of this fundamental and powerful argument. They had believed the words of the uneducated foreign missionaries who had for a long time closed their eyes to advances in the theological world. There is a saying, "A blind man is not afraid of a snake." The Christian church at the time was above all else like a blind man that does not fear a snake. Any number of people with the capacity to think of the future prospects of the church could have seen, as the magazine *Shinri* did, the signs of a dreadful revolution that would shake the foundations of the so-called orthodox church.

Strangely, at about the time that these new principles came to Japan, even in the orthodox church the sound of the new theology was becoming louder. In the July 1889 edition of *Rikugō zasshi*, Kozaki Hiromichi argued about biblical inspiration. The orthodox church taught that the Bible was written by God through the hands of the disciples, but Kozaki argued that, contrary to the teachings of the orthodox church, the significance of inspiration was simply that the writers received the influence of God.

In 1880, Uemura Masahisa, who had just returned from a tour of the West, supported the idea of the creation of a new doctrine and argued that the existing doctrine should be reformed. Yokoi Tokio, who had also just returned from a world trip, advocated progressiveness too. There was doubt about the doctrine of the trinity. There was difficulty with the doctrine of atonement. People laughed at the idea of the virgin birth. At the time, *Rikugō zasshi*, which was recognized by society at large as a general organ of the Christian church, fell completely into the hands of the progressive faction, and it vigorously called for a new theology. In June 1891 there was the publication of a small book by Kanamori Tsūrin entitled *The Present Church in Japan and the Church of the Future*. This pamphlet clearly illuminated the teachings of the Higher Criticism faction. Kanamori took a very direct approach and destroyed the orthodox faction.

At the time, Kozaki, Uemura, Yokoi, and Kanamori were respected by the church and were considered scholarly figures. They were the most important people in making *Rikugō zasshi* a wonderful journal at a time when it was the only beacon for young people belonging to the Christian church. Without these men, *Rikugō zasshi* would have been nothing but blank paper. Whether their style was slow-paced or fast, whether they argued for rapid change or gradual change, all equally supported the new theology and expressed support for it. This really swept the church into stormy seas and into great change. After this, the Christian church completely lost its clarity of thought. Some of these people had an interest in Confucianism and tried to harmonize Christianity with Confucianism, or they brandished some superficial knowledge of Zen.

The publication of Yokoi Tokio's *Problems of Christianity in Our Country* came in 1894. The table of contents was as follows:

1. The Old Theology Must Be Destroyed
2. A New Theology Must Be Constructed
3. The Christianity of the Church Must Be the Teachings of Christ Himself

4. The Ultimate Origin of All Things Is Unknowable

5. God is Manifest in All Things. Christ is the Manifestation of God

6. We Humans Cannot Escape from Our Positions As Humans. The thing we clearly perceive as human beings, however, is the responsibility to develop and to put into practice an ethical ideal. This responsibility of ours is most definite and most noble. We revere the place of God and believe in God, and the needs humans have for a moral sense must be based on this.

This explanation was certainly nothing new. Even if you read just one page of theological history, you will know that these kinds of pantheist thinkers often made a noise in the church. In the final analysis, their thinking was philosophical not scientific. Their thinking was half-baked and contained innumerable contradictions. In trying to open up a new theological world, their thinking was too crude and superficial. As a result of their attempts in this area, however, they stirred up the Christian church, which had belatedly come in contact with the new Western theological thought. In this regard, their work must be considered a landmark in Japanese intellectual history.

28

THEOLOGICAL DISPUTES II

In this way there was a rebellion by those within the church who advocated the new theology. I deeply regret that at the time there were very few among those claiming to adhere to the old theology who raised the banner of belief and entered the theological battle. According to my own recollections of the time, Uemura Masahisa at one point showed support for the progressive faction but had a change of heart and returned to the old faith and fought well as a general in the orthodox faction. Uchimura Kanzō[78] also stood on the side of orthodoxy and wrote bold and decisive essays on its behalf, even though he publicly stated that he believed in Darwinism.

Other people, however, including even those who were elders within the church at the time, largely avoided contact with theological problems. Alternatively, they offered some excuse and would not fight with the progressive faction. They stayed inside the walls of the church and did nothing except utter a few words

---

78. Uchimura Kanzō (1861–1930) was born in Tokyo but was educated at the Sapporo Agricultural College (now Hokkaido University), where he came under the influence of Christianity. He lived in America for a number of years, and after his return he worked as a teacher in a number of different schools. In 1891 he was forced to resign from his position at the First High School after he hesitated to bow before a signed copy of the Imperial Rescript on Education. His action was interpreted as showing a lack of respect for the imperial family, and it greatly stimulated attacks on Christians who were accused of being unpatriotic. Following the incident Uchimura earned a living as a writer, and by 1897 his critical essays had earned him the position of senior editor of the influential newspaper the *Yorozu chōhō*.

of complaint. They did not wish to enter the spiritual battle to meet another person's challenge and to strengthen the walls of belief. This confused people's hearts, but the leaders of the church saw no reason to try to assist. This was cowardly behavior, was it not?

I must admit that the writer of the present book became involved in theological problems as a supporter of the old faith through the pages of the Methodist paper *Gokyō*.[79] I was indignant at the attitude of the elders in the church. To speak honestly, I had few resources available relating to theological knowledge. I believed that the way of dealing with the opposition could only be understood if the reason for defending the faith was made clear within the church itself. I knew when I entered the theological battlefield that I was weak in troops and munitions. The area of faith, however, had become a battlefield. Even though I had only one bow and one spear, I could not refuse to go to the front of the battle. For this reason, I fought for the orthodox faction. At the time, I thought the field of theology was very confused and the prospect before us was very dark. This, however, is not an unusual situation. It is recorded in the history of the church that the church has often been attacked by dreadful criticism and scepticism.

After rainy winds, however, there are always clear skies. After unstable mud has been swept away, firm rocks remain. People experienced the pain of uncertainty in theology, but theology is not faith. On the one hand, there was the Textual Criticism school and the Higher Criticism school. On the other hand, there was the Oxford Movement. One side emphasized science; the other side emphasized ancient texts. Historical research is a way of reaching religion. History, however, is not directly religion. The Tübingen school studied the Christ of Christianity. The church, however, was established on the basis of its own view of Christ. From the point of view of the historian, Christ was above all else a historical phenomenon: one link in history. From the point of view of a believer, he was a person who was God. You

---

79. *Gokyō* (Defender of the Faith) was a journal established by the Methodist Church in 1891.

could say he was God, he was a great man, he was a person. This is merely a belief people have toward something they have encountered. When there is a comet, there is a light in the sky. The physicist simply takes this as a physical light. If a poet sees it, however, it has a meaning beyond this.

Religion is the experience of the human heart. It is a mystical interpretation. The historical Jesus depicted by historians is nothing more than the external form of something the religious person sees. The religious person must see the inner Christ through his own view of the universe and his own mystic experience. Peter saw him this way. Paul saw him this way too. The ancient Church with its deep faith also saw him in this way. So-called Christianity is nothing but the belief of the church toward Christ. This is completely outside the bounds of critical research and historical criticism, is it not?

Religion is like poetry. It is not something that can be arrived at through logical analysis. The ordinary person cannot interpret the life of a genius. If someone tries to do research on religion, he must have a religious life within a researcher's heart. The so-called advocates of the new theology did not attain a profound level of understanding on this point. Historical and scientific research was the beginning and the end of their methodology. It was the basis of their argument. Looking back on them now, we must recognize that they ran to youthful extremes. At the same time, however, they felt compelled to enter the theological battlefield. They felt they had no other choice. In the end this was wasted effort. On the whole, the so-called orthodox faction was fearful and dealt neither with the attack of the Tübingen school nor with the challenge of the new theology. They did not go along with those of a different opinion, nor did they fight with them. They did not work to support their own faith, nor did they study the theories of their opponents, work out a suitable compromise, and try to make a new faith. They uselessly tried to dress up the external appearance of the orthodox church. I must say that this was really irresponsible behavior.

For these reasons, belief within the church declined. There was a tendency for the intellectual class to feel contempt for the beliefs of the church they belonged to themselves. No development could be seen for the next ten years. I do not say that I had the foresight to anticipate this. If, however, the so-called elders had advanced and entered the theological disputes; fought well and settled the hearts of the people; raised the banner of belief and made things clear; dealt with those things that needed to be dealt with, and separated those things that needed to be separated—if all these had been done, then we would have seen free spiritual interaction within the church. The church elders did not do this, however, so the tendency toward passivity came into being within the church. It is to be regretted that the church completely lost both the unique character it had had until about 1887 and its intense faith.

29

THE ATTITUDE OF THE CHURCH TOWARD THE NEW THEOLOGY—UNFAIRNESS

The fact that this theological dispute occurred is not something that should be regarded as regrettable for the church. This is because it could have been the preparation for the establishment of a firmer base for the church and for its renewal. Even if the Tübingen school had been completely victorious, this would not have meant the destruction of Christianity. Just as the advance of science does not destroy poetry, so criticism or textual analysis, no matter how detailed, does not destroy religion. Knowledge is concerned with phenomena, but going beyond phenomena is the territory of religion. Even the people in the Tübingen school respected the religious elements in the Bible and the church as before. Basically, the Tübingen school appeared to support Christianity against the criticism and textual analysis of the German Pure Reason faction.

Thus, the theological disputes, no matter what extreme they may have run to, were not something to be feared. In the final analysis, there was another reason why the Japanese church alone lost its vigor: the majority of the people within the church cooperated with the foreign missionaries, and, as a result, their attitude toward theological problems lacked fairness. The same fetters that were revealed in the case of Niijima Jō caused equal suffering to other missionaries in the Japanese church. The majority of them received the assistance of foreign missionary societies to support their missionary work. The majority of the foreign missionary societies, however, persisted as before in the so-called traditional principles. With the appearance of the new theology, the missionaries of the Christian church fell into a situation where their spirits were poisoned. If they expressed their beliefs freely, the source of funds for their missionary work would dry up. Is it not a fair criticism to say they were vague about their beliefs because of their livelihoods? We cannot doubt that they were unable to freely, boldly, and honestly enter theological disputes because of the position they were in. This is really something Japanese thinkers should be ashamed of. With the appearance of the new theology, the church was unable to act in an appropriate way. This was the reason the church finally lost its vigor.

Freedom to debate is not something that will destroy the truth. The church declined because of the theological dispute, but not because there was freedom to debate. It was because thinkers in the church were restrained from free debate and therefore adopted a vague attitude. It is to be deeply regretted that this is a blot on the history of the Japanese church that cannot be removed.

30

THE CONSERVATIVE REACTION I

I would now like to move on and record the position of the Christian church in opposition to the conservative reaction that occurred at the same time as the theological dispute.

I have already described how Count Inoue and Prince Itō encouraged Westernization as a part of the policy to get treaty revisions and how this policy failed. I have also described how even though the attempted treaty revision failed, people's hearts were greatly enlightened by Western scholarship and culture, and foreign culture continued to be imported as before. As a result, public opinion was very well disposed toward Christianity. A reaction, however, finally had to come. The policy of Westernization had its initial motivation in foreign policy. Therefore, when it became no longer necessary, it inevitably entered a period where it lost vitality. An interest in national, as opposed to international, topics had appeared some years before, and gradually a portion of the people began to change. I know that in the university and among government officials, from about 1884 on, there was an interest in the so-called German style of things. What is the German style? If you say the Manchester school's[80] laissez-faire and internationalist spirit was English in style, then you can say the

---

80. The "Manchester school" was a group including John Bright (1811–89) and Richard Cobden (1804–65) that espoused laissez-faire economic policies.

German style was an emphasis on the system and law-making and an emphasis on the statist spirit.

In 1885, the Itō cabinet was established and Mori Arinori became the Minister of Education. He represented a strange phenomenon among the education ministers of modern Japan. He always took an extreme position, and was always too far ahead of his time. As soon as the feudal system fell, he advocated abolishing swords, and he advocated equal rights for men and women. Not only did he advocate the abolition of the national language and the use of English in education, but he tried to make his own lifestyle like that of a Westerner. He was the first leaf to fall, showing that autumn had come to the world. The changes in his way of thinking always failed because they came too early. If you look at the things he did ten years later, however, he was always at the vanguard of his age. He always anticipated the age to come. In 1885, when he became minister of education, he devoted himself completely to national education. This is a point everyone who discusses the intellectual history of the time must pay attention to. Mori said:

> There are three things that are important in education now: the maintenance of dignity, obedience, and a feeling of sympathy for the people. These three things are attained through military education. This is because military education makes people serious. It makes people obey the orders of their superiors. A brotherly affection develops among the ranks. Devoting oneself to national duty creates these three characteristics.

For Mori, the student studied for the state, and schools produced people for the state. There was a time when he taught that, first of all, society must be free. That was during the time when he taught world civilization, the thought of Mill and Spencer, and that the state was a necessary evil. When he became minister of education, however, he advocated the creation of loyal citizens for the state. For the creation of loyal citizens, he believed, military education was necessary. In the educational world, from the university at the top, down to the elementary school at the bottom, the backbone of education was the acquisition of the characteristics of the soldier. Elementary school students were made to carry wooden guns on their shoulders, and students in teacher training schools were made to live as though they were in barracks. This behavior was completely lacking in common sense, was it not?

This, however, was just Mori Arinori doing what Mori Arinori had to do. He was really forecasting through himself the coming nationalist reaction (against the West). This was still insufficient, however, to turn around the swiftly flowing current of Westernization. Finally, the Inoue plan failed, and for the first time society began to feel a dislike for Westernization. In 1888, the magazine *Nihonjin* appeared.[81] This gave voice in literary circles to the nationalist reaction. One group followed another. If even small streams combine, they form a great river. When society grew tired of elitist progressivism, of imitated Western civilization, and of English-style political debating, a time of prosperity for the reactionaries came. There is a proverb that says: "A little cloud on the mountain peak indicates a torrential rain at the base of the mountain." Statism was like a cloudburst that poured down on the Japanese intellectual world. It was the church, however, that experienced the greatest pain.

---

81. *Nihonjin* was a journal established by Miyake Setsurei, Shiga Shigetaka, and others that first appeared in 1888. It stressed traditional Japanese values in opposition to the superficial imitation of the West popular at the time.

31

THE CONSERVATIVE REACTION II

Here I must request the attention of the reader! The conservative reaction that took place in 1881 or 1882 was nothing more than the revival of Chinese studies. The conservative reaction that occurred from 1887 onward, however, was nothing less than the rise of national consciousness.

Of course, even in this later conservative reaction, Buddhist priests in mountain temples, as well as old Shintoists and Confucianists who longed for the past, were all pleased and threw themselves into it. It is also a fact that the main branch of the faction that brought about this reaction were people with an understanding of Western civilization. They saw the unification of Germany in 1871 as a landmark in intellectual history. They breathed in the spirit of the nationalist movements in the various Western countries that occurred at about the same time. Since 1871 they had seen the Japanese government any number of times try and fail to revise the treaties. They were indignant at the lack of self-respect of the Japanese people. They believed that it was a dangerous tendency to try to make Japanese thought and customs the same as those of the West. They saw that the various Western countries worked to support the uniqueness of their people in the areas of language and literature, manners and customs. On this point, they clearly preached to the people. They said, "We must not imitate." They said, "We must preserve the national essence." They said, "We must cultivate the unique Japanese spirit of loyalty and patriotism." They changed the main current of thought. Finally, the so-called nationalist spirit was victorious. (At the time, those who did not sympathize with them called this a conservative spirit.) The intellectual balance had for a long time inclined toward freedom and internationalism, but now it began to incline in the other direction. No matter what the society, when the current of thought begins to flow with the force of water gushing from a spring, normal conditions are swept away and victims appear unnecessarily. The first victim of this poisoned spirit that ordinary people noticed was Uchimura Kanzō, the enthusiastic Christian and honest patriot. Even now people still remember the Uchimura Incident.

Before this, on 11 February 1889, the day the constitution was proclaimed, the then minister of education, Mori Arinori, was killed by an assassin. There were rumors before this that Mori had committed an act of disrespect at Ise Shrine. The assassin believed these rumors and, thinking that such a person should not have responsibility for national culture, stabbed him with a death-defying spirit. At the time, the *Kokumin no tomo* commented on this amazing event. It argued that Mori was a conservative and that the person who stabbed Mori had the conservative spirit Mori had encouraged. It was amazing, the journal continued, that Mori had strangely become the victim of the conservative spirit, and it was regrettable that there were such contradictions in human affairs. If it was as the reporter of the *Kokumin no tomo* wrote, then Mori was the first victim of contradictions in the conservative spirit and Uchimura was the second. Even if at that time there was no great gap between Uchimura and the Christians, he was an enthusiastic patriot because he most bitterly hated the foreign missionaries.

I have a recollection of the time. In 1889, on the emperor's birthday, I heard a lecture by Uchimura at the Tōyō Eiwa Gakkō[82] in Azabu. At that time he pointed to a chrysanthemum that adorned the podium and said that the flower was one of nature's special blessings to Japan. It is a famous flower unique to Japan. He raised his voice and said, "Ladies and gentlemen, look out of the win-

---

82. Tōyō Eiwa Gakkō was a school for boys established in 1884 by missionaries from the Canadian Methodist Church.

dow and see Mount Fuji, which rises in the western sky. This is also splendid scenery bestowed upon our country by heaven. Students, please remember, however, that in Japan, the greatest and most mysterious thing, which surpasses all things in the world, is, in reality, our Imperial Household." He said, "Our Imperial Household, like heaven and earth, has no end. It should be the only pride of the Japanese people." His quiet attitude, his expression of sincerity, and his appearance deeply moved the audience.

He was a scientist. He had a great interest in Western literature. He was, however, a patriot. At the time, he loved to read the Bible, the *Taiheiki*,[83] and Shakespeare. He loved to read the *Taiheiki* and burned with the spirit of loyalty. In this regard, he was pure Japanese, and he belonged to the conservative party. Strangely, however, he became the victim of the conservative reaction.

He was a teacher at the First Higher School, and on the emperor's birthday of the following year, he hesitated to worship before a portrait of the emperor, as it had religious significance. For this reason people regarded him as disrespectful. He was completely banished from the educational world and thrown into adversity. Public opinion had been suspicious of the attitude of Christians for a long time. As a result of Uchimura's action, the stigma of disloyalty and lack of patriotism was also assigned to Christianity, and people cursed Christianity for this.

In December of that year, the magazine *Tensoku* (this was published by Katō Hiroyuki) reported the following account:

> Recently I heard that in a meeting in Nagoya there was a certain person called Ariga who was regarded as a moralist. He was a believer in Christianity and he had a deep faith in the church for a short period of time. Suddenly, however, he left the church. When I asked the reason, he said, "Unfortunately, on the third of last month on the emperor's birthday, I saw that a fan with the flag of a certain country had been put above the portrait of our emperor. I thought this was a sign of great

83. The *Taiheiki* (Chronicle of the Great Peace) is a work dating from around 1370, which gives an account of both the origins and conflict between the northern and southern courts in the period 1318–67.

> disrespect and removed the fan and earnestly warned the minister. At the time of the celebration of the opening of the Diet, there was a similar event, and so I have withdrawn from the church."

This is nothing more than one article that shows the anti-Christian trend of the time.

In January 1892 there was an inauguration ceremony for the principal of Kumamoto English School. Among the teachers was a person called Okumura Teijirō. He discussed philanthropy, and in one phrase he said that in his eyes there was no such thing as the state. The people of the conservative party picked up on this phrase and criticized it severely, and thus the governor of Kumamoto Prefecture ordered the school to dismiss Mr. Okumura. I must say that this was a second Uchimura Incident.

The waves increased and the flood of the nationalist reaction gained strength. War cries could be heard outside the walls of the church demanding that "the heresy [Christianity] must be swept out of Japan." The newspapers and magazines that influenced the thought of the times competed in trying to vilify Christianity.

In the *Nihon shinbun*[84] of 29 August of this year there was the following item:

> A certain elementary school student in Yatsushiro, Higo, seeing a portrait of the emperor hanging in Classroom One, said, "What's that?" and knocked it down with his fan. The teacher quickly called him and asked him the reason. He said proudly, "I heard from the missionary I believe in that we should not worship anyone but God, and thus I knocked it down." There was a great uproar in the region and the pupil was ordered to leave the school.

In *Eiri jiyū shinbun*[85] of 12 October of the following year, there appeared:

---

84. The *Nihon shinbun* was a newspaper established by Kuga Katsunan and others in 1889.
85. The *Eiri jiyū shinbun* was a newspaper established in 1882 that had connections with the Liberal Party.

In the prisons of our country before the promulgation of the constitution, a priest of the Shinshu sect usually acted as a prison chaplain and preached to the prisoners for an allowance. Since the promulgation of the constitution in February 1889, there has been freedom of belief. Since then, at Sorachi Prison, the prison warden Oinoue Terusaki has banned Buddhism, and there has been a Christian prison chaplain. He preached to the prisoners, but I do not know what the results were. With the reorganization of the government, however, the various prisons in Hokkaido were organized with Kabato as the main prison, and Sorachi, Kushiro, and Abashiri as local prisons. Oinoue was the head warden, so Christianity was preached to the prisoners. Until now, every year on New Year morning, the prisoners were made to worship a portrait of the emperor. On New Year's Day this year, however, Oinoue ordered the local prisons to remove the image of the emperor and to put it in a corner of the storeroom. The prisoners were not made to worship it. In questioning why the prisoners do this, it was found to be the result of the belief in Christianity. What an act of disrespect for the head warden of a prison!

This is just one example.

The spirit of the times was most clearly expressed in the essay made public by Inoue Tetsujirō in 1893 entitled *The Collision Between Education and Religion*. The main points of Inoue's arguments were:

1. Education in our country must be based on the Imperial Rescript on Education.
2. The Imperial Rescript is statist and based on filial piety. Christianity is based on internationalism not statism. It teaches that there should be no discrimination in love, and thus it does not teach loyalty to the state. It teaches that above our lord there is God and Christ, and thus it is opposed to loyalty and filial piety.
3. For this reason religion and reason are in collision.

Apart from the one point of defining his own so-called statism on the basis of the Imperial Rescript on Education, this argument does not go beyond that of Yasui Sokken. His knowledge of Christianity was extremely crude. Throughout all his writing, it is clear that he had no knowledge at all of the theological dispute that existed within the church at the time. Also, because his criticism of the Bible was not at all scholarly, he completely departed from the Bible's overall purpose, from the overall and balanced relationships contained in the Bible, and from its true spirit. Through selected quotations he summarized the Bible, and on this basis he built up his criticism of Christianity. At the time, he was professor of literature and had, more or less, the position of a representative of the Imperial University. For this reason his arguments had great influence throughout the Japanese educational world, and the larger part of the educational world, came to see Christianity as the enemy.

32

INOUE TETSUJIRŌ AND THE
CHRISTIAN CHURCH

In any discussion of modern Japanese intellectual history, Inoue
Tetsujirō is one person who cannot be overlooked. Of course, he
does not have the power of originality characteristic of great philosophers. He does not have the kind of bold spirit necessary to
change the thinking of a generation. His scholarship is extremely
shallow, and his personality is also not one that we would necessarily admire. He is in certain regards a pragmatist. In the intellectual world, he is a teacher who teaches only subjects of topical
interest, but he is always active. As opposed to other professors at
the Imperial University, who are like hermits and stay cooped up
within the university walls, he always publicly criticizes the times.
He does not shun the world. He does not forget the world. He is
someone who always criticizes things that are happening at the
time. He is known in the world more as a critic of contemporary
trends of thought than as a professor at the Imperial University. I
take him up as a subject because he is one of the personalities in
modern Japanese intellectual history.

Inoue spent a long time at government expense in Germany as an exchange student, and soon after he returned he tried
to give a lecture at the university entitled *The Present Condition of
Western Philosophy* (1891). This lecture, however, did not necessarily add to his reputation as a philosopher. In this lecture, he
took empiricist philosophy and pessimistic philosophy as the main-
streams of modern thought. He took Comte, Spencer, and

Hartman[86] as representatives of these schools and argued that they were the greatest philosophers of modern times.

He introduced Hartman to the Japanese people simply because he had just newly returned from overseas, did he not? That is, Hartman published *Unconscious Philosophy* at the age of forty-seven, just two years before Inoue gave this lecture. In this way, he taught subjects only of topical interest in the intellectual world. In his lecture, Inoue called the pessimistic philosophy the most sublime form of thought and explained that the pantheist view of ignoring the responsibility of individual intention was the most scientific and rational form of thought. In this way, he had no weight as a philosopher. To speak honestly, he had no clear understanding of the condition of Western philosophy at the time. He argued that there was Hegel; that as a reaction to Hegel, empiricism came into being; and, as a reaction against empiricism, there appeared the teachings of Newman.[87] He said, "The progress of philosophy can be traced back to Kant, and the progress of political thought can be traced back to Aristotle." He did not know about the great trend toward the revival of Kant. He was doing nothing more than showing off his new knowledge to an audience that expected to hear something new from someone who had just returned from overseas.

The rise of nationalist feeling, however, was a good opportunity for him. He quickly made public his *The Collision Between Religion and Education* and added his own blow to the Japanese church. His personality is most clearly shown in his style of arguing. The articles he selected in relationship to the Uchimura Incident were from the Buddhist Shinshu sect journal *Ryochikai zasshi*. This journal had always shown a fierce hatred of Christianity. The magazines and newspapers from which he selected articles concerning the disloyalty and lack of filial piety of Christians were publications like *Tensoku, Nihon shinbun,* and the *Kyūshū*

---

86. Auguste Comte (1798–1857) was a French sociologist who founded the positivist school of thought. Herbert Spencer (1820–1903) was an English philosopher who sought to unify all knowledge on the basis of the principle of evolution. Eduard von Hartman (1842–1906) was a German philosopher and psychologist.

87. John Henry Newman (1801–90) was a historian, theologian, and leader of the Oxford movement.

nichinichi shinbun. If they did not regard Christianity as their enemy, then they were at least contemptuous of it.

He began his argument as if he did not know that the magazines and newspapers he quoted tended to put the worst possible interpretation on the actions of Christians. He wrote as if he did not know that anti-Christian feelings had arisen in the schools because the Ministry of Education had said that it hated Christianity, and it had warned teachers about entering the church. He acted as if he did not know it was a time when Buddhist priests were jealous of Christianity and when Buddhists falsely vilified Christians because of their prejudice. Without hesitation or consideration, he used defamatory materials in anti-Christian newspapers and magazines as a firm basis of fact upon which the truth could be established. In this regard, he completely lacked the fairness and detachment of a scholar.

With regard to the study of Christianity, he was almost a complete layman so that in his essay there are often laughable mistakes. For example, there is the following paragraph in his essay:

> As I have explained, Jesus was weak in patriotic feeling. This is clear from his cold answer that people must pay tax to the Roman government. Mr. Yokoi has taken the same answer as proof that he taught loyalty. I can never agree with Mr. Yokoi's defense. Can we regard Christ simply saying we must pay tax to the Roman government as the principle of loyalty? Does loyalty to the ruler stop at paying tax to the government without delay? Also, there is not one piece of evidence that Christ was a patriot, but there are passages that show that he lacked patriotic feeling. Yokoi expressed the idea that the Jewish state was in decline and it was difficult to do anything, and thus Christ simply said you must pay your tax to the Roman government. If the country had been living under one ruler, we do not know what kind of meritorious deeds would have been performed. At the time, however, the Jewish state had a king called Herod. What kind of loyalty did Christ have toward Herod? Even if Herod was a tyrant, did Christ try to dissuade him from this? Again, did he correct this? Did he present some plan concerning this?

There is clear proof in this paragraph that Inoue did not know that Herod, rather than being a Jewish patriot, was a member of the Roman party and was hated as a traitor. If he did not know even this obvious fact from Christ's life, what qualifications did he have to discuss Christianity?

His method was not to criticize Christian texts historically. He did not study what Christianity was as a whole. His argument was nothing more than simply taking a few phrases from Christian texts and saying that what they taught was contrary to patriotism. In this way, he found fault with Christian individualism because it was not statist.

If we use this method, however, could the two religions of Buddhism and Confucianism avoid his denunciation? Buddhism is divided into various groups, and their arguments are varied but, in a word, they find salvation in the individual soul. They speak of enlightenment, awakening, nirvana, and a land of peace after death. Are not all these things related to the individual soul? The *Greater Learning* says, "The way of greater learning is to make clear illustrious virtue, to be familiar with the people, and to end in the supreme good." This so-called "making clear the illustrious virtue, being familiar with the people, and ending in supreme good" is all related to the individual spirit, is it not? For this reason it says, "Knowing to stop, being settled, after being settled, being quiet"—this is first of all governing oneself on the basis of ethics.

Also, the teachings of the various sages of the world were the products of a time when the idea of the state did not exist or else it was very weak. As for recognizing the existence of Inoue's so-called statism in such an age, this is merely to try to create something that did not exist. This is really an empty theory.

Inoue wrote:

> The purpose of the Imperial Rescript on Education is to govern oneself for the state. Filial piety to one's parents, friendship for brothers and sisters, this is all for the state. We must offer ourselves to the service of the state and we must die for our emperor.

This is not necessarily something we should criticize. The idea of national education should be something like this, should it not? He argues, however, that because national education is like this, then valuing the independence of the conscience that places trust in religion is contrary to the idea of the Imperial Rescript. This is really an empty theory without basis.

Where there is no freedom of conscience, there is no sincerity. Where there is no sincerity, there is no feeling. Where there is no feeling, how can there be patriotism and filial piety? In short, his method kills itself. His attitude toward his subject is one of intemperance, and he completely lacks the attitude of a scholar.

In the opening sentences of his essay, Inoue wrote the following: "Even though for a long time I have had an opinion concerning the relationship between religion and education, this is a serious matter and I have not wished to discuss it." Is this the way a scholar writes? What kind of pomposity is this? In meeting the attack of Takahashi Gorō,[88] however, he quickly changed his attitude and requested a truce. He wrote Takahashi the following open letter:

> 28 March
>
> To Takahashi Gorō
>
> Dear Sir,
>
> *The Collision Between Religion and Education*, which I published several months ago in *Kyōiku jiron*, was an amplification of a brief talk. It is still incomplete. In the quotations there are some uncertainties. I plan to correct these and make this available as a pamphlet. For this purpose, your criticism is useful for me.
>
> Yours sincerely,
>
> Inoue Tetsujirō

This is a kind of joke, is it not? If you judge this matter as a whole, you cannot say that this essay was successful for Inoue. The fame of a person who was a teacher at the university, a professor with a reputation, and a German-trained scholar, however, together with the thought of the nationalist reaction, gave his essay sharp teeth. The majority of educators saw this essay as an all-

---

88. Takahashi Gorō (1856–1935) was a Christian scholar with considerable linguistic talent who knew English, French, German, Greek, and Latin. In addition to his many translations, he also wrote extensively about Buddhism.

encompassing principle, and they burnt fiercely with anti-Christian emotions. Persecution of Christians began in schools. School teachers did not confess openly that they were Christians. In a country school, there were people who threw objects through the windows of a church at the instigation of a teacher. Even in Nagasaki in 1899, there was this kind of anti-Christian attitude among a section of elementary school teachers. Because most of them had read Inoue's essay and had been influenced by it, I feel we cannot take his influence lightly.

33

THE VICTORY OF THE SO-CALLED
STATIST EDUCATION

Christians could not remain quiet concerning Inoue's essay. The magazine of the Christian youth group, *Kirisutokyō seinen*,[89] argued that education and religion had different foundations—one was built on the state and the other lay in the universe—and thus there was no collision between them. Honda Yōichi, Yokoi Tokio, Maruyama Tsuichi, Uemura Masahisa, Ōnishi Hajime, Ishikawa Kizaburō, Maeda Chotarō, and so on—all put forward various kinds of arguments.

The defense of Takahashi Gorō was especially brilliant. Neither Takahashi nor Inoue, however, were people who had a systematic knowledge of Christianity. If we evaluate them from the perspective of today, they were both kindred spirits with regard to research on Christianity in that neither of them were serious scholars of Christianity. Neither of them had knowledge of recent biblical criticism. With regard to Christianity, both of them adopted the method of selective quotation and argued philosophically, not historically. Also, as a critique of Inoue's essay, Takahashi's work lacked any really penetrating insights, and he was a long way from the scholarly attitude of Ōnishi. Takahashi's essays were highly acclaimed, however, because they were published, and they had the greatest influence of the works put out by the *Kokumin no tomo* at the time. In reality, however, in response to

---

89. *Kirisutokyō seinen* (Young Christians) was first published in 1893 and played a supporting role to the *Rikugō zasshi*.

Inoue's argument that Christianity was unpatriotic and lacking in loyalty and filial piety based on selective quotations from here and there in the Bible, Takahashi's argument was nothing more than saying that this was not the case, on the basis of selective quotations from here and there in the Bible. The argument did not have any particular value. Public opinion was surprised by the exaggeration of this boastful scholarship, and this dispute became known as "the debate between Inoue and Takahashi."

In this way, Christians were engaged in a fierce defense of their faith. Public opinion in the educational world, however, glorified Inoue and could hardly be moved from the idea that education must be based on statism and that Christianity was opposed to the idea of the Imperial Rescript on Education.

34

THE STAGNATION OF THE CHURCH

Thus the church, which was torn internally by theological disputes and externally rejected by educators, finally fell into a state of complete stagnation. From 1892 or 1893 hardly any progress could be seen. In 1902, a small pamphlet was published in Tokyo that said:

> The Christian church has been in decline and stagnant for a long time. The number of believers is the same as ten years ago, and the number of churches is also the same. I do not wish to argue whether the church is stagnant or not on the basis of a head count, but I think it is sufficient proof that the internal life of the church is in decline.

Not only could one not see the signs of the progress that had existed in the first fifteen or sixteen years of the Japanese church, but weakness was apparent at every turn. The next most striking thing was that so-called famous people gradually separated themselves from the church. Kanamori Tsūrin was an outstanding student of Niijima Jō and was once a leader of the church. He left early and entered the business world. Before we were aware of it, Yokoi Tokio had become a politician. Ōnishi Hajime,[90] an educated gentleman and representative of the young progressive

90. Ōnishi Hajime (1864–1900) graduated from the Theology Department of Dōshisha College and then studied philosophy at Tokyo University. He taught at Tōkyō Senmon Gakkō and also helped edit *Rikugō zasshi*. He strongly opposed the nationalism of Inoue Tetsujirō and believed that religion transcended the state.

church, distanced himself from the church. Instead of going to church and listening to a sermon in order to cultivate his spirituality, he came to a stage where he stayed home and read *The Collected Works of Emerson*. The most talented people from among the Christian clergymen who had graduated from Dōshisha changed their profession. There were also many similar examples from among the theological students who had been educated in the so-called missionary schools of the various denominations. With regard to talented people, the church gradually came to feel a sense of loneliness, and missionary work came to be despised by talented young people.

Uchimura Kanzō, an independent missionary outside the sphere of the foreign missionaries, seeing talented people giving up evangelical work like this, severely criticized them for their lack of sincerity. Some of the foreign missionaries, seeing the large number of Japanese students who had been raised in their schools and who did not carry out missionary work as they had promised, secretly grumbled at the insincerity of the Japanese. We cannot attribute this failure, however, solely to their insincerity. In reality, there were weaknesses within the church itself that caused talented people in society to separate themselves from the church. This fact was expressed strikingly in the decline in numbers and quality of the young people who entered the theological departments of the missionary schools with the intention of doing evangelical work in the future. The result was that the church lost many talented people, the number of people who attended went down, and there was a loss of vigor and a decline in belief.

Why did the church, which for a long time had embraced such high hopes for the future, fall into decline like this? If we trace it back simply to the theological disputes, the opposition of educators, and the ignorance of foreign missionaries, we cannot say that we have understood the whole of the matter. I think there were two other great causes: progress in the lives of the people and trends in the overseas churches.

35

THE RISE OF THE BUSINESS WORLD
AND CHRISTIANITY

Why do I say that advances in the lives of the people in Japan contributed to the stagnation of the church? In 1891, the *Kokumin no tomo* described the rise of the business world in the following way:

> We know that a commercially oriented society is coming when we see the so-called strong young men—who formerly wore high *geta* and brandished walking sticks—walking around carrying briefcases and wearing new style business suits advertising they are businessmen.

This really showed the signs of the time. The wealth and standard of living of the Japanese people progressed in leaps and bounds since the Restoration, and without parallel in the world.

In 1889, foreign trade was worth 1.4 billion yen; in 1891, 1.9 billion; in 1900, 5 billion. Businessmen were for a long time subordinate to the samurai, but there was a change in society and they reversed roles. They are now in a position where they control the government. The business world can pay comparatively large amounts of money, and thus talented people are inevitably attracted. In the past, those young people who did not wish to become politicians went into literature. Those who did not wish to go into literature threw themselves into the religious world. This was the reason that many talented people gathered in the religious world at that time. The trend of the times, however, changed. The business world was vast, but it was full of ripe crops that beckoned young people. It is said that, "When the field turns golden, it is time to harvest. There are few to harvest but much to be harvested." This was not the condition of the Japanese spiritual world but rather the condition of the business world. In the Christian world, there was a lot of work in becoming a teacher and few rewards. There were many evil abuses when people had to be subservient to the foreign missionaries, and thus they welcomed the value of a salary. Talented people in society did not head for the church but went into the business world. When one considered human nature, this was not unreasonable. For this reason, I maintain that advances in the lives of the people was one reason for the stagnation of the Christian church.

36

TRENDS IN THE CHURCHES OVERSEAS AND THE INFLUENCE ON THE JAPANESE CHURCH

Development in means of transportation accompanied the development of civilization. With the development of transportation, the distance between Japan and the world has become much shorter. This is the most striking fact in modern Japanese intellectual history.

For the Japanese church, this has meant that it has developed at the same pace as the various churches in the West. In this regard, we cannot hide the fact that the second half of the nineteenth century was a period of stagnation for the church in the West. There were isolated areas of success that ran against the general trend. In one place there may have been the flickering flame of renewed belief, and in another place there may have been support for the old style of belief as a result of meditation on the Scriptures. Speaking generally about the trend in all countries, however, there was a decline in the number of people attending church; a decline in the number of people who read the Bible; a decline in the number of people who observed the Sabbath; and a decline in the number of people who believed in the basic tenets of the church, such as the virgin birth, miracles, and the ascension of Christ. It is also clear that there was a lack of certainty about the doctrine of the trinity.

In 1899 or 1900 Professor Adolf von Harnack[91] gave a series of lectures at Berlin University. He argued that the essence of

91. Adolf von Harnack (1851–1930) was a German Protestant Church historian and theologian.

Christianity was not so much Christ himself, as his teachings. It was like saying a theory of Christ was not Christianity. In 1901, the Russian literary master Tolstoy wrote in his novel *Resurrection* that "I believe in God. God in love is the origin of all things. I believe that the teachings of the man Christ are the most clear and the most comprehensive interpretation of God's purpose. I think it is a great blasphemy, however, to consider Christ as God and to worship Christ as God." Both of these cases are evidence of this trend. Even among the French Roman Catholics, who must be regarded as conservative, there were those who publicly used the results of the Higher Criticism school. Even at King's College in England the religious test that had historically long been part of the school system was abolished in 1902. Seeing these things, people knew that a great revolution was approaching the Christian church.

The conditions in foreign countries were like this. The Japanese church alone could not support the old position, could it? I think that the trend in the churches overseas was the other great reason for the stagnation of the Japanese church.

37

WE SHOULD NOT BE PESSIMISTIC
ABOUT THE FUTURE OF THE CHURCH

For these reasons, does the Japanese church have no future? Why should it be so? We should not be pessimistic about the future of the church. Look! In the last few years, the Japanese spiritual world has shown signs of revival in its religious aspects, has it not? I cannot avoid seeing this trend, and so I will discuss some of the signs of the times.

A. THE BANKRUPTCY OF STATIST EDUCATION

Statist education was preached by Inoue and others. It was enforced by officials of the Ministry of Education and that ministry was almost completely controlled by graduates of the university. Even if there is no need to debate the objective of trying to make good citizens, the methods they used were too mechanical, and they oppressed the real ability of the students. For this reason, even though these people were successful in oppressing the feeble Christian church, they could not satisfy the young people who entered the schools. The statist educators had one principle and this they extended to schools throughout the country. Their ideal was to create people who were loyal and patriotic.

This, however, was nothing more than a vision. The young people of Japan listened to teachers give lectures in nasal tones about patriotism and filial piety. At first, they greeted these with a serious attitude. As they were repeated over and over again, however, they began to yawn loudly. No matter what principle a doctrine might have, they could not endure having it poured into them from outside. Those who had spirit rose up and fought against this. Takayama Chogyū,[92] a protégé of the Imperial University, upon leaving the university came to expound a theory of the aesthetic life. Tobari Chikufu[93] studied Nietzsche and attacked the principles of morality. In this way, students rebelled against the so-called statist education.

The trend toward self-indulgence continued for a long time. During the Russo-Japanese War, a reporter of the *Kokumin shinbun* wrote:

> Young people, when they attain self-consciousness as individuals, lose a national consciousness or at least a part of it. Those with a sense of individualism incline toward materialism and become the so-called "worshippers of money," and the comparatively healthy ones become the so-called "enthusiastic, successful, young people." Those who incline toward spirituality become the students of disappointment, despair, discouragement, and world-weariness. Those with comparative health study about the "problem of life," and others become megalomaniacs with distorted fantasies. Some young people are more moved by criticism of a play than by the great war in Manchuria.

In the children's story *Togi monogatari* there is the following tale. A hen had several eggs and kept them warm under her wing in the expectation that they would hatch. When she saw them hatch, contrary to her plan, they were baby ducks and competed with each other in racing toward the water. The compassionate hen, seeing this, could not bear the sorrow. Are not the advocates and supporters of the so-called statist education like this hen? They expected that loyal and patriotic people would be born from under the wings of their educational institutions. But Look! Among

---

92. Takayama Chogyū (1871–1902) was a literary critic and novelist who published many works in the journals *Teikoku bungaku* and *Taiyō*. He vigorously advocated Japanese nationalism following the Sino-Japanese War and later became an admirer of the German philosopher Nietzsche. His brand of romantic individualism was extremely popular in the 1890s and early 1900s.
93. Tobari Chikufu (1873–1955) was a scholar of German literature who first introduced the work of Nietzsche to Japan.

those who have been raised in this system, an extreme form of individualism has been created. They write poems of love, of stars, and violets. Their ideal is merely to fulfil their own desires, and they care nothing for the existence of the state.

Here the advocates of statist education have felt the bankruptcy of their own principles. Even if they do not confess it publicly, they have changed their attitude. Up until now they have excluded religion from schools, but now they welcome religious people. In 1901 or 1902 Inoue Tetsujirō made public his wish to start a new religion. In his later years, the Ministry of Education official Sawayanagi Masatarō[94] in his book *On Teachers* recognized that people with religious faith had contributed to the state and society. He advised teachers themselves as part of their training to believe in religion. Tanimoto Tomeri,[95] a disciple of Inoue Tetsujirō, who had contributed to the vilification of Christianity, also argued for the compatibility of religion and education when he talked about Ōnishi Hajime at the Okayama Church in the same year. Do not these examples all equally show that the advocates of statist education themselves had thrown away their old doctrines?

In the last few years in the Japanese spiritual world, one can see a collision between authority and talent, between the state and the individual. In 1900, the old Fukuzawa Yukichi met with students of Keiō College and lectured on how the principles of independence and self-respect were the basis of morality. He sent his students all over the country to try to spread this doctrine. This was the voice of opposition to statist education from a giant

---

94. Sawayanagi Masatarō (1865–1927) was a graduate of Tokyo University and served as vice-minister of education, first president of Tohoku University, and president of Kyoto University. He was an advocate of the New Education movement that emphasized the individuality and the initiative of the student in opposition to the standardized education of the state-controlled school system as it existed in the mid-Meiji period.

95. Tanimoto Tomeri (1867–1946) was educated at Tokyo University and later taught at Kyoto University and Bukkyō Daigaku (now Ryukoku University). At first he advocated the educational theories of the German philosopher and educator Johann F. Herbart (1776–1841). He later turned against Herbart's ideas and advocated education for the benefit of the state. In the Taishō period he again changed his views and supported the idea of education for the benefit of the individual.

who had done great deeds in the history of Japanese education. He opposed contemporary educational theories that used the authority of the state to mechanically try to oppress the human spirit.

Of course, the supporters of bureaucratic learning who considered statist education to be an unmovable principle of heaven could not help but protest. Inoue Tetsujirō, who never remained silent, criticized Fukuzawa's theory in the following way:

> Without obedience it is difficult for a society to exist for even a day. The reason society exists is because of obedience. If we really put into practice independence and self-respect, the result would be the self-destruction of people and the destruction of order in society. We cannot escape the fact that these two things are one. Relationships between people joined together on the basis of the division of labor make up an organic group. This is called society. Human beings cannot help but form societies because of their natural characteristics. From time immemorial man has been a social creature. This is really the case. Independence and self-respect with no obedience would cause a disturbance in the foundations of society. This is a commonplace of eighteenth-century thought.

At the time, the government newspaper *Tōkyō nichinichi shinbun* said the standard of moral education must be uniform throughout the country. The Fukuzawa group did not agree. They did not believe in the government establishing a doctrine of moral education and using it to try to dominate people's hearts. They believed that in the past such attempts had not been successful and had done nothing more than harm society. They knew that students brought up in bureaucratic learning would grow tired of the mechanical, uniform education. This is the reason they advocated independence and self-respect in opposition to the mechanical statist education.

Virtue is not isolated. It always has a neighbor. Historical laws do not permit the existence of one single phenomenon. The voices of those who valued independence and self-respect and those who valued ability were both raised against statist education. Takayama and Tobari were nothing more than the products of this trend. The reaction toward individualism ran to an extreme.

Literary figures who were graduates of the Imperial University proclaimed openly and in writing that young people should drink alcohol and should visit the red-light district.

Along with the rise of this kind of sensualism and together with the development of the self-awareness of the individual, however, there is also an entry into the world of mysticism. There is the discovery of the truth of selfless love. There are those who say, "We have seen God." In extreme cases there are even people who say, "I can predict the future." In the Japanese spiritual world at the moment, there is a tendency to think of people as individuals rather than debating the value of people as citizens. Together with this comes the revival of religious needs. This is a good opportunity for the Christian church to awaken from its sleep of the last few years.

B. The Rise of Socialism

I have already explained how advances in the living conditions of the Japanese people caused competition among talented people and how they were drawn into the business world. The result was that there was a decline in the number of young people who wished to become clergymen.

All forces, however, arrive at a limit. Young Japanese people diligently pursued material satisfaction, but they began to fear that their desires were inadequate with regard to the structure of society. The present capitalist system, which is based on individualism and freedom, increased the wealth of the people as a whole, day after day. The people who received a share of these riches, however, were only from the wealthy class. Socialism or social reformism had long been a stream in Western thought, but now it has entered the door of the Japanese empire. Katayama Sen was the forerunner of this trend. In 1901, Ōi Kentaro, a fugitive from the political world, said, "I plan to throw myself into the labor problem. There is nothing else I will think about in the political world." He raised a banner demanding assistance for workers and wished to fight a social war. Count Itagaki, having retired from the political world, also made it known that the task of his retirement would be to carry out the reform of society. Yano Ryūkei also argued the need to reform society.

Abe Isoo, Kinoshita Naoe, Sakai Toshihiko, and Kōtoku Shūsui are all socialists.[96] In Tokyo and Kyoto universities there are those who express support for the German academic Socialists.[97] There are state socialists and Christian socialists. Their beliefs do not all contain the same principles, but they all have one thing in common. Compared to the period when the freedom and individualism of the Manchester school was popular, there is a comparatively greater concern for and greater sympathy for the interests of the individual as a member of society as a whole. This trend will arouse the attention of people with regard to the fundamental Christian principle, "God is the father and all men are brothers." I must say that this is a good sign for the future prospects of the church. Also, young people know the weakness of the material satisfaction they can derive from the present system, and they will return to the religious world and do some evangeli-

---

96. Abe Isoo (1865–1949) was educated at Dōshisha College where he came under the influence of Niijima Jō. He spent the period from 1891 until 1895 in the United States, and in 1903 he became a professor at Waseda University. He was one of the founders of the Shakai Shugi Kenkyūkai (Society for the Study of Socialism) and Japan's first socialist party, the Shakai Minshuto (Socialist Democratic Party). Kinoshita Naoe (1869–1937) was a novelist, socialist, and Christian pacifist. He graduated from the Tōkyō Senmon Gakkō and later worked as a journalist first in his native Nagano Province and then later in Tokyo. He strongly opposed both the Sino-Japanese and Russo-Japanese Wars and also wrote critically of social injustice, including the Ashio Copper Mine Incident. In later life he gave up involvement in social issues and retired to a life of meditation. Sakai Toshihiko (1871–1933) worked with Uchimura Kanzō and Kōtoku Shūsui on the newspaper *Yorozu chōhō* and left with them at the time of the Russo-Japanese War as a result of the paper's prowar stance. He began to publish the *Heimin shinbun* with Kōtoku, and in 1904 the two men translated and published Karl Marx's *Communist Manifesto*. As a result, the newspaper was closed down by the government. Before joining the *Heimin shinbun*, Kōtoku Shūsui (1871–1911) participated in the Freedom and Popular Rights movement and the Shakai Shugi Kenkyūkai. After the closure of the *Heimin shinbun* Kōtoku spent some time in prison, and following that went to the United States. After his return he was disillusioned with the idea of working within the system and became an advocate of "direct action." He was executed in 1911 as a result of his involvement in a plot to assassinate the Meiji emperor, although his precise degree of involvement in the plan is unclear.
97. This is a reference to German academic economists such as Adolph Wagner (1835–1917), who believed that the state should actively intervene in society in order to ameliorate the consequences of class conflict.

cal work. The old feeling of sympathy has also come back into existence among the talented people who went into the industrial world. This is another reason why we should be optimistic about the future prospects of the Japanese church.

C. Changes in International Relations

In the last ten years, Japan's international position has experienced an astonishing change. In international law, Japan has entered the group of powers. It has a responsibility and right to speak on all world problems. To put this in other words, Japan now stands on the side of the masters who control the world. This is an age in which a great change must take place in the spiritual condition of the Japanese people. There must be a great difference in the thought of the people in an age when Japan was an isolated country cooped up in the East, diligently working to preserve its independence, and in an age in which Japan is a power with the right to vote in the court that judges international law cases. Now, the Japanese people must become world leaders on the basis of a philosophy and religion that shows sympathy for all the people in the world. This is a good opportunity for the Japanese people to once again investigate Christianity, which for a long time has been the faith of the civilized world.

38

THE CHRISTIAN CHURCH OF THE FUTURE

For these reasons, I believe there will be a period when the Christian church will revive with renewed energy.

Why will a revival come? I cannot forecast the future. How can I say I know this? The general trend is not difficult to guess. In my view, there has been a complete victory for the liberal faction in Christian theology in Japan. There is Uemura Masahisa's *Fukuin shinpō* and Uchimura Kanzō's *Shinkibo*[98] that support the beliefs of the orthodox faction, but they are like isolated castles being defended against a huge surrounding army. Free inquiry based on science and history has flooded the church. For the liberal faction, Ebina Danjō's magazine *Shinjin* is very successful.[99] The editor of the Japanese Methodist magazine *Gokyō*, Takagi Mizutarō,[100] publicly stated that free inquiry must not be abandoned. He has taken the view that any position theoretically possible should be welcomed, no matter what its doctrinal basis. This is not simply the position of the Japanese theological world. From 1870 onward, this trend has run through the Western theological world, and, in fact, this kind of movement is a great world trend.

---

98. *Fukuin shinpō* was a Christian journal first published in 1891 under the title *Fukuin shūhō*. Publication was temporarily suspended after the Uchimura Incident as it was regarded as being an antigovernment publication.
99. *Shinjin* (New People) first appeared in 1900 and dealt with contemporary problems as well as political, literary, and scholarly topics.
100. Takagi Mizutarō (1864–1921) was a theologian and educator who played a leading role in the development of the Methodist Church in Japan.

The plan for today should be nothing more than to boldly and clearly carry out free investigation, to wait for the return of calm and the establishment of a new theological foundation. Together with this spirit of free inquiry, there has been a movement to free the church from the hands of foreign missionaries. This is definitely a powerful development. For example, the result of the discussion between the American Board and the representatives of the General Council of the United Churches of Japan last year was that, from 2 January this year, churches that had received the financial support of foreign missionaries would become affiliated with the Combined Japanese Church Missionary Society. In the same period, all churches in Japan, including the large churches, planned to become independent. Supporters of the Japanese Methodist church plan to make the church financially and administratively independent in the next five years. These are examples of this trend.

In this way, the Japanese people, by studying by themselves, by interpreting by themselves, and by establishing a new theology that satisfies their own needs, will have their own church. The problems of the Japanese church will arrive at a complete resolution. I earnestly desire that members of the Japanese church put their strength into this.

BIBLIOGRAPHY

Collections and Reprint Editions of Yamaji's Work

Aizan bunshū. Edited by Uchiyama Shōzō. Tokyo: Min'yūsha, 1917.

Ashikaga Takauji. Tokyo: Genkōsha, 1909. Reprint, Tokyo: Iwanami Shoten, 1949.

Dokuritsu hyōron, 1–7. Tokyo: Dokuritsu Hyōronsha, 1903–10. Reprint, Tokyo: Misuzu Shobō, 1987.

Jinsei, mei ka tsumi ka. Edited by Ishigami Ryōhei and Ishigami Hiroko. Tokyo: Ei Shobō, 1985.

Kirisutokyō hyōron: Nihon jinminshi. Tokyo: Iwanami Shoten, 1966.

Kitamura Tōkoku, Yamaji Aizan shū. *Gendai Nihon bungaku taikei* 6. Tokyo: Chikuma Shobō, 1969.

Minamoto no Yoritomo: Jidai daihyō Nihon eiyūden. Tokyo: Heibonsha, 1987.

Tokugawa Ieyasu. Tokyo: Iwanami Shoten, 1985.

Tokutomi Sohō, Yamaji Aizan. *Nihon no chōmei* 40, edited by Sumiya Mikio. Tokyo: Chūō Kōronsha, 1971.

Yamaji Aizan denki senshū. 10 vols. Rpt. Tokyo: Nihon Zusho Sentaa, 1998.

Yamaji Aizan shiron shū. Tokyo: Misuzu Shobō, 1958.

Yamaji Aizan shū. *Meiji bungaku zenshū* 35, edited by Ōkubo Toshiaki. Tokyo: Chikuma Shobō, 1965.

Yamaji Aizan shū I & II. *Min'yūsha shisō bungaku sōsho* 2 & 3, edited by Oka Toshirō. Tokyo: Sanichi Shobō, 1983, 1985.

Secondary Sources

Abe, Yoshiya. "From Prohibition to Toleration: Japanese Government Views Regarding Christianity, 1854–1973." *Japanese Journal of Religious Studies* 5 (June–September 1978): 107–38.

Ballhatchet, Helen. "The Religion of the West versus the Science of the West: The Evolution Controversy in Late Nineteenth Century Japan." In *Japan and Christianity: Impacts and Responses*, edited by John Breen and Mark Williams, 107–21. Basingstoke: Macmillan Press Ltd., 1996.

_____. "Confucianism and Christianity in Meiji Japan: The Case of Kozaki Hiromichi." *Journal of the Royal Asiatic Society* 2 (1988): 349–69.

Best, Ernest E. *Christian Faith and Cultural Crisis: The Japanese Case.* Leiden: E. J. Brill, 1966.

Blacker, Carmen. *The Japanese Enlightenment: A Study of the Writings of Fukuzawa Yukichi.* Cambridge: Cambridge University Press, 1964.

Burkman, Thomas W. "The Urakami Incident and the Struggle for Religious Toleration in Early Meiji Japan." *Japanese Journal of Religious Studies* 1 (June–September 1974): 143–216.

Cary, Frank. *History of Christianity in Japan.* Tokyo: Kyo Bun Kwan, 1959.

Cary, Otis. *A History of Christianity in Japan: Roman Catholic, Greek Orthodox, and Protestant Missions.* 2 vols. New York: Fleming H. Revell, 1909.

Davis, Winston. "The Civil Theology of Inoue Tetsujirō." *Japanese Journal of Religious Studies* 3 (March 1976): 5–40.

Dohi Akio. *Nihon Purotesutanto Kirisutokyō shiron.* Tokyo: Kyōbunkan, 1987.

_____. *Nihon Purotesutanto Kirisutokyō shi.* Tokyo: Shinkyō Shuppansha, 1982.

_____. "Christianity in Japan." In *Christianity in Asia* vol. 1, *North East Asia,* edited by T. K. Thomas, 30–66. Singapore: Christian Conference of Asia, 1979.

_____. "Kozaki Hiromichi: shisō to kōdō." *Kirisutokyō shakai mondai kenkyū* 16/17 (1970.3): 1–37.

_____. "Nihon saisho no Purotesutanto kyōkai." *Kirisutokyō shakai mondai kenkyū* 8 (1964.4): 24–33.

Dōshisha Daigaku Jinbun Kagaku Kenkyūjo (Kirisutokyō Shakai Mondai Kenkyūkai). *Nihon Purotesutanto sho kyōha shi no kenkyū.* Tokyo: Kyōbunkan, 1997.

_____. *Matsumoto Tairo ni okeru Kirisutokyō: Iguchi Kigenji to Kensei Gijuku.* Kyoto: Domeiya Shuppan, 1979.

Drummond, Richard H. *A History of Christianity in Japan.* Grand Rapids, MI: William B. Eerdmans Publishing Company, 1971.

Duus, Peter. "Whig History, Japanese Style: The Min'yūsha Historians and the Meiji Restoration." *Journal of Asian Studies* 33. 3 (May 1974): 415–36.

Ebara Sensei Den Hensan Iinkai. *Ebara Soroku sensei den.* Tokyo: Ebara Sensei Den Hensan Iinkai, 1924.

Ebisawa Arimichi and Ōuchi Saburō. *Nihon Kirisutokyō shi.* Tokyo: Nihon Kirisutokyōdan Shuppankyoku, 1971.

Gagan, Rosemary R. *A Sensitive Independence: Canadian Methodist Women Missionaries in Canada and the Orient, 1881–1925.* Montreal: McGill-Queen's University Press, 1992.

Germany, Charles H. *Protestant Theologies in Modern Japan: A History of Dominant Theological Currents From 1920–1960.* Tokyo: IISR Press, 1965.

Gonoi Takashi. *Nihon Kirisutokyō shi.* Tokyo: Yoshikawa Kōbunkan, 1990.

Howes, John F. "Japanese Christians and American Missionaries." In *Changing Japanese Attitudes Toward Modernization,* edited by Marius B. Jansen, 337–68. Princeton: Princeton University Press, 1965.

Iglehart, Charles. *A Century of Protestant Christianity in Japan.* Rutland, VT & Tokyo: Charles E. Tuttle, 1959.

Ion, A. Hamish. "Edward Warren Clark and the Formation of the Shizuoka and Koishikawa Christian Bands (1871–1879)." In *Foreign Employees in Nineteenth-Century Japan*, edited by Edward R. Beauchamp and Akira Iriye, 171–89. Boulder, Colorado: Westview Press, 1990.

————. *The Cross and the Rising Sun: The Canadian Protestant Missionary Movement in the Japanese Empire. 1872–1931*. Waterloo: Wilfrid Laurier University Press, 1990.

————. "Edward Warren Clark and Early Meiji Japan: A Case Study of Cultural Contact." *Modern Asian Studies* 11. 4 (1977): 557–72.

Howes, John. "Japan's Enigma: The Young Uchimura Kanzō." Ph.D. diss., Columbia University, 1965.

Igarashi Akio. "Kyūbakushin no Meiji Ishin." In *Iwanami kōza Nihon tsūshi dai 16 kan kindai 1*, edited by Iwanami Nihon Tsūshi: Henshū Iinkai, 310–24. Tokyo: Iwanami Shoten, 1994.

Iida Hiroshi. *Shizuoka ken eigaku shi*. Tokyo: Kōdansha, 1967.

Imanaka Kanshi. "Yamaji Aizan kenkyū ni: Fukuroi no fūrai dendoshi." *Shizuoka-ken kindaishi kenkyū* 12 (1986): 60–68.

————. "Yamaji Aizan no shisō to Kirisutokyō, 'Nihon shisō shi ni okeru Kirisutokyō no ichi'." *Kirisutokyō shakai mondai kenkyū* 11 (1967.3): 169–96.

Isono Naohide. "Shinkaron no Nihon e no dōnyū." In *Kyōdō kenkyū Mosu to Nihon*, edited by Moriya Takeshi, 295–325. Tokyo: Shogakkan, 1988.

Ishigami Ryōhei and Ishigami Hiroko. "Kaisetsu." In *Yamaji Aizan jinsei, mei ka tsumi ka*, 115–227. Tokyo: Eii Shobō, 1985.

Itō Yushi and Graham Squires. "A Reconsideration of the Myth of Japanese Uniqueness: Rewriting Nihonjinron." In *Japanese Society Today*, edited by Kotaku Ishido and David Myers, 147–60. Rockhampton: Central Queensland University Press, 1995.

————. "Approaches to Japanese History in the Late Meiji Period: Yamaji Aizan and Inoue Tetsujiro." *New Zealand Journal of East Asian Studies* 1.1 (1993): 111-29.

Kawasaki Tsukasa. "Tōhoku. Aizan. Meiseki. Kandō: Oitachi to Shukkai." In *Nihon Purotesutanto shi no shosō*, edited by Takahashi Masao, 142–74. Ageo City: Sei Gakuin Daigaku Shuppankai, 1995.

————. "Yamaji Aizan kenkyū—daini no gokyō Shizuoka." *Shizuoka-ken kindaishi kenkyū* 4 (1980): 62–80.

Kinmonth, Earl H. *The Self-Made Man in Meiji Japanese Thought: From Samurai to Salaryman*. Berkeley: University of California Press, 1981.

————. "Nakamura Keiu and Samuel Smiles: A Victorian Confucian and a Confucian Victorian." *American Historical Review* (June 1980): 535–56.

Kishimoto Hideo, ed. *Japanese Religion in the Meiji Era*. Translated by J. F. Howes. Tokyo: Obunsha, 1956.

Ko T. "Kaisetsu, Yamaji Aizan ni tsuite." In *Yamaji Aizan shiron shū*, 455–85. Tokyo: Misuzu Shobō, 1958.

Kogawa Keiji and Ji Myon Kwan, eds. *Ni kan Kirisutokyō kankei shiryō 1876–1922*. Tokyo: Shinkyō Shuppansha, 1984.

Kohiyama Rui. *Amerika fujin senkyōshi: Rainichi no haikei to sono eikyō*. Tokyo: Tokyo Daigaku Shuppankai, 1992.

Kosaka Masaki, ed. *Japanese Thought in the Meiji Era*. Translated by D. Abosch. Tokyo: Pan-Pacific Press, 1958.

Kozaki Hiromichi. *Reminiscences of Seventy Years: The Autobiography of a Japanese Pastor*. Translated by Kozaki Nariaki. Tokyo: Christian Literature Society of Japan, Kyo Bun Kwan, 1934.

————. *Nanajūnen no kaiko*. Tokyo: Kaiseibo Shashoten, 1928.

Kudo Eiichi. *Nihon Kirisutokyō shakai keizei shi kenkyū: Meiji shoki o chūshin toshite*. Tokyo: Shinkyō Shuppansha, 1980.

————. *Nihon shakai to Purotesutanto dendō—Meiji ki Purotesutanto shi no shakai keizei shi kenkyū*. Tokyo: Nihon Kirisutokyōdan Shuppanbu, 1970.

"Kumamoto Bando no kenkyū tokushu." *Kirisutokyō shakai mondai kenkyū* 7 (1963.4).

Kuranaga Takashi. *Hiraiwa Yoshiyasu den*. Tokyo: Kyōbunkan, 1938.

Lande, Aasulv. *Meiji Protestantism in History and Historiography: A Comparative Study of Japanese and Western Interpretation of Early Protestantism in Japan*. Frankfurt am Main: Verlag Peter Lang, 1989.

Maruyama Masao. *Thought and Behaviour in Modern Japanese Politics*. London: Oxford University Press, 1963.

Neuss, Margaret. "On the Political Thinking of Yamaji Aizan." In *Tradition and Modern Japan*, edited by P. G. O'Neill, 93–101. Kent: Paul Norbury Publications, 1981.

————. "Zur Rolle der Heldenbiographien im Geschichtsbild Miyake Setsureis und Yamaji Aizans." *Oriens Extremus* 25.1 (1978): 1–44.

Nihon Kirisutokyō Rekishi Dai Jiten Henshū Iinkai, ed. *Nihon Kirisutokyō rekishi dai jiten*. Tokyo: Kyōbunkan, 1988.

Nihon Kirisutokyōdan Shizuoka Kyōkai. *Nihon Kirisutokyōdan Shizuoka kyōkai hachijūnen shi*. Shizuoka: Nihon Kirisutokyōdan Shizuoka Kyōkai, 1959.

Nippon Mesojisutō Shizuoka Kyōkai. *Nippon mesojisutō Shizuoka kyōkai rokujūnen shi*. Shizuoka: Nippon Mesojisutō Shizuoka Kyōkai, 1936.

Nishiyama Shigeru. "Shimosa Fukuda seikokai no keisei to tenkai [shita]." *Shingaku no koe* 19.2 (1973.6): 21–39.

————. "Shimosa Fukuda seikokai no keisei to tenkai (jo)." *Shingaku no koe* 18.2 (1972.6): 10–27.

Notehelfer, Fred G. *American Samurai: Captain L. L. Janes and Japan*. Princeton: Princeton University Press, 1985.

————. "Leroy Lansing Janes and the American Board." In *Nihon no kindaika to Kirisutokyō*, edited by Dōshisha Daigaku Jinbun Kagaku Kenkyūjo Kirisutokyō Shakai Mondai Kenkyūkai. Tokyo: Shinkyō Shuppansha, 1973.

Ogihara Takashi. *Nakamura Keiu to Meiji keimō shisō*. Tokyo: Waseda Daigaku Shuppansha, 1984.

Ohama Tetsuya. *Meiji Kirisutokyō kaishi no kenkyū*. Tokyo: Yoshikawa Kōbunkan, 1979.

Oka Toshirō. *Yamaji Aizan, shironka to seijironka no aida*. Tokyo: Kenbun Shuppan, 1998.

————. "Min'yūsha shiron ni okeru rekishi to seiji." *Nihon shisōshi* 30 (1988): 35–49.

————. "Yamaji Aizan." In *Kindai Nihon no janarisuto*, edited by Tanaka Hiroshi, 279–94. Tokyo: Ochanomizu Shobō, 1987.

_____. "Kaisetsu." In *Yamaji Aizan shū II*, edited by Oka Toshirō, 455–61. Tokyo: San'ichi Shobō, 1985.

_____. "Yamaji Aizan to *Gokyō:* Aizan shuhitsu jidai no *Gokyō* ronsetsu mokuroku." *Hokudai hōgaku ronshū* 36.12 (1985): 563–74.

_____. "Shizuoka jiken to Yamaji Aizan." *Shizuoka ken kindaishi kenkyūkai kaihō* (1983. 12): 1–3.

_____. "Meiji Nihon no shakai teikokushugi: Yamaji Aizan no kokkazō." In *Nenpō seijigaku, 1982*, edited by Nihon Seiji Gakkai, 107–27. Tokyo: Iwanami Shoten, 1983.

_____. "Yamaji Aizan to jaanarizumu." In *Kindai Nihon ni okeru jaanarizumu no seijiteki kinō*, edited by Tanaka Hiroshi, 3–36. Tokyo: Ochanomizu Shobō, 1982.

_____. "Yamaji Aizan kenkyū josetsu 'wakudeki' to 'gyoko.'" *Hokudai hōgaku ronshū*. 25.4 (1975): 333–63; 26.1 (1976): 37–106; 26.4 (1976): 691–720.

Ōkubo Toshiaki. *Sabakuha rongi*. Tokyo: Yoshikawa Kōbunkan, 1986.

Osawa Saburō. *Nihon Purotesutanto shi kenkyū*. Tokyo: Tōkai Daigaku Shuppankai, 1964.

Ōta Aito. *Meiji Kirisutokyō no ryūiki: Shizuoka bando to bakushintachi*. Tokyo: Tsukiji Shokan, 1979.

Ōta Yuzō. *Eigo to Nihonjin*. Tokyo: Kōdansha, 1995.

Ozawa Eichi. *Kindai Nihon no shigakushi no kenkyū Meiji hen*. Tokyo: Yoshikawa Kōbunkan, 1969.

Pierson, John. *Tokutomi Sohō 1863–1957: A Journalist for Modern Japan*. Princeton: Princeton University Press, 1980.

Powles, Cyril H. "Foreign Missionaries and Japanese Culture in the Late Nineteenth Century: Four Patterns of Approach." *North East Asia Journal of Theology* (1969): 14–28.

Powell, Irene. *Writers and Society in Modern Japan*. Tokyo: Kodansha International, 1983.

Roden, Donald. *School Days in Imperial Japan: A Study in the Culture of a Student Elite*. Berkeley: University of California Press, 1980.

Saba Wataru, ed. *Uemura Masahisa to sono jidai*. 8 vols. Tokyo: Kyōbunkan, 1967.

Sakamoto Takao. "Yamaji Aizan no shisō—toku ni zenhanki no katsudo o chūshin to shite." *Gakushuin Daigaku hōgakubu kenkyū nenpō* 20 (1985): 105–311.

_____. "Yamaji Aizan no seiji shisō." *Gakushuin Daigaku hōgakubu kenkyū nenpō* 21 (1986): 103–309.

_____. *Yamaji Aizan*. Tokyo: Yoshikawa Kōbunkan, 1988.

Scheiner, Irwin. *Christian Converts and Social Protest in Meiji Japan*. Berkeley and Los Angeles: University of California Press, 1970.

Schwantes, Robert S. "Christianity Versus Science: A Conflict of Ideas in Meiji Japan." *The Far Eastern Quarterly* 12.2 (February 1953): 123–32.

Shiono Kazuo. *Nippon kumiai kyōkai shi kenkyū josetsu*. Tokyo: Shinkyō Shuppansha, 1995.

Shiori Takashi. "Nagano jidai no Yamaji Aizan: Purudamu jiken o chūshin ni shite." In *Nihon Purotesutanto shi no shosō*, edited by Takahashi Masao, 175–95. Saitama-ken: Sei Gakuin Daigaku Shuppen Kai, 1995.

Shizuoka Eiwa Jo Gakuin Hachijūnen Shi Hensan Iinkai. *Shizuoka Eiwa Jo Gakuin hachijūnen shi*. Shizuoka: Shizuoka Eiwa Jo Gakuin, 1971.

Sugii Mutsurō. *Meiji shoki Kirisutokyō no kenkyū*. Kyoto: Dōshisha Shuppan, 1984.

————. "Kumamoto Bando. Dōshisha to bungaku: 'Dōshisha bungaku' no taido." *Bungaku* 47.4 (1979): 167–86.

————. "Tokutomi Sohō ni okeru Kirisutokyō." *Kirisutokyō shakai mondai kenkyū* 18 (1971.3): 27–99.

Sumiya Mikio. *Nihon Purotesutanto shiron*. Tokyo: Shinkyō Shuppansha, 1983.

————. *Nihon no shakai shisō kindaika to Kirisutokyō*. Tokyo: Tokyo Daigaku Shuppankai, 1968.

————. *Kindai Nihon no keisei to Kirisutokyō*. Tokyo: Shinkyō Shuppansha, 1962.

————. *Nihon shakai to Kirisutokyō*. Tokyo: Tōkyō Daigaku Shuppankai, 1954.

Takahashi Masao. *Nakamura Keiu*. Tokyo: Yoshikawa Hiroshi Bunkan, 1967.

Thelle, N. R. *Buddhism and Christianity in Japan: From Conflict to Dialogue, 1854–1899*. Honolulu: University of Hawaii Press, 1987.

Thomas, Winburn T. *Protestant Beginnings in Japan: The First Three Decades 1859–1889*. Rutland, VT & Tokyo: Charles E. Tuttle, 1959.

Tokutomi Sohō. *The Future Japan*. Translated and edited by Vinh Sinh, with Matsuzawa Hiroaki and Nicholas Wickenden. Edmonton: University of Alberta Press, 1989.

Totman, Conrad. *The Collapse of the Tokugawa Bakufu, 1862–1868*. Honolulu: University of Hawaii Press, 1980.

Tōyō Eiwa Jo Gakuin Hyakūnen Shi Hensan Jikkō Iinkai, ed. *Tōyō Eiwa Jo Gakuin hyakūnen shi*. Tokyo: Tōyō Eiwa Jo Gakuin Hyakūnen Shi Hensan Jikkō Iinkai, 1984.

Tsukada Osamu. *Shoki Nippon seikōkai no keisei to imai judō*. Tokyo: Seikōkai Shuppan, 1992.

————. "Nippon Seikōkai kito sho ni okeru *Tenno no tame* no sho kito no keifu." *Kirisutokyō* 25 (1983): 69–92.

Williams, Mark. "From out of the Depths: The Japanese Literary Response to Christianity." In *Japan and Christianity: Impacts and Responses*, edited by John Breen and Mark Williams, 156–74. Basingstoke: Macmillan Press Ltd., 1995.

Yamamoto Yukinori. "Rikugō zasshi to Hiraiwa Yoshiyasu." In *Rikugō zasshi no kenkyū*. 2 vols., edited by Dōshisha Daigaku Jinbun Kagaku Kenkyūjo Hen, 1:233–57. Tokyo: Kyōbunkan, 1984.

————. "Yasui Sokken no *Benmō* to Meiji shonen no Kirisutokyōkai." *Kirisutokyō shakai mondai kenkyū* 32 (March 1984): 68–128.

————. "Yamaji Aizan to Kirisutokyō: Meiji niju nendai o chūshin to shite." *Kirisutokyō shakai mondai kenkyū* 28 (December 1977): 102–62.

Yamazaki Masakazu and Miyakawa Toru. "Inoue Tetsujirō: The Man and his Works." *Philosophical Studies of Japan* 7 (Japan National Commission for Unesco) (1966): 11–25.

INDEX

ABOUT THE AUTHORS

Graham Squires is Lecturer in Japanese in the Department of Modern Languages, University of Newcastle, Australia.

A. Hamish Ion is Professor in the Department of History, Royal Military College of Canada, Kingston, Ontario.